THE GLOW OF THE OIL LAMP

A CHILDHOOD REMEMBERED IN TRANQUILLITY

Art. P. O'Dálaigh

Cover cartoon by Eamon McCreave O.S.M.

© Copyright 2004 Art P. O'Dalaigh. All rights reserved.

No part of this publication may be reproduced, stored in a retrieval system, or transmitted, in any form or by any means, electronic, mechanical, photocopying, recording, or otherwise, without the written prior permission of the author.

Printed in Victoria, Canada

Note for Librarians: a cataloguing record for this book that includes Dewey Classification and US Library of Congress numbers is available from the National Library of Canada. The complete cataloguing record can be obtained from the National Library's online database at:
www.nlc-bnc.ca/amicus/index-e.html
ISBN 1-4120-2428-5

TRAFFORD

This book was published on-demand in cooperation with Trafford Publishing. On-demand publishing is a unique process and service of making a book available for retail sale to the public taking advantage of on-demand manufacturing and Internet marketing. On-demand publishing includes promotions, retail sales, manufacturing, order fulfilment, accounting and collecting royalties on behalf of the author.

Suite 6E, 2333 Government St., Victoria, B.C. V8T 4P4, CANADA
Phone 250-383-6864   Toll-free 1-888-232-4444 (Canada & US)
Fax 250-383-6804   E-mail sales@trafford.com   Web site www.trafford.com
TRAFFORD PUBLISHING IS A DIVISION OF TRAFFORD HOLDINGS LTD.
Trafford Catalogue #04-0256   www.trafford.com/robots/04-0256.html

10   9   8   7   6   5   4   3   2

For my wife, Maureen,
at whose instigation I publish this memoir.

ACKNOWLEDGEMENTS

There are a number of people I have to thank for encouraging and urging me to publish this record of my days of childhood. My wife, Maureen, has been unceasing in her desire to see the book come to fruition, and to her must go my deepest thanks, and I hope that she enjoys it. I am indebted to Tommy Jordan for giving me permission to put some of his exploits before the world, and I would like to take this chance to say a word of appreciation also for his lifelong friendship and help. To the many people around Eglish, Benburb and the Moy, who have told me in the last few years that I have a gift for telling good stories, I want to express my appreciation. I hope that in reading this book they will get much satisfaction and enjoyment. Thanks too, to my daughter Sinead, who helped out when the computer and I did not see eye to eye. Her sister Grainne helped with the proof reading and gave some useful suggestions, and to her I also wish to express my deepest thanks. On the other hand I dread to think how my son, Michael will use the material contained herein, to continue the abuse of his long- suffering father.

A very special word of deep appreciation must go to Mr. Aidan McKavanagh, who agreed to edit the book and bring it to its final format. It is said that if one wants a job done, one should always go and ask a busy man, and in Aidan's case that is certainly true. I hope that he is satisfied with the fruits of his endeavours.

Once again I must mention the editor of my last book, Fifty Years in Ireland, Mr. Martin O'Brien. Martin read parts of very early versions of this book, and encouraged me to proceed with it, so to him too, I am deeply grateful. Fr. Eamon McCreave O.S.M. painted the cartoon of Benburb, which is used on the cover. I appreciate very much the fact that he and his fellow Servites have allowed me to use it.

I am delighted that I discovered the Trafford on-demand publishing service. They certainly offer a unique and comprehensive service, which up until now, people like myself could only dream about. Courtesy and understanding are their hallmark, and I found them a joy to work with.

Art P. O'Dálaigh
Sessiamagaroll
February 2004

CONTENTS

INTRODUCTION 9

Chapter 1
I GO FORTH, BLINDLY 13

Chapter 2
SESSIAGH : A TOWNLAND LIKE NO OTHER 18

Chapter 3
THE PRIDE OF HAVING A TIN ROOF 26

Chapter 4
BESSIE THE GOAT AND TRIMMER THE DOG 38

Chapter 5
A NEW BEGINNING 54

Chapter 6
A PLAGUE OF HENS AND TURKEYS 61

Chapter 7
THE WHITE OWL'S NEST 73

Chapter 8
BREAKING INTO BARNEY'S 84

THE SACRED CYCLE 95

Chapter 9
TROUBLE IN TAXIS 97

Chapter 10
THE GLOW OF THE OIL LAMP 108

Chapter 11
THE WAKE OF ADOLF HITLER 115

Chapter 12
DA'S DEVOTIONS..131

Chapter 13
A FEW DAYS MITCHING............................155

Chapter 14
A WEE BIT OF A SHAKING 162

Chapter15
THE TALE OF A ROANEY COW 173

Chapter 16
THE ROAD TO THE FAIR 181

Chapter 17
THE HOUSE AMONG THE TREES 203

Chapter 18
INVOLVEMENT IN A BATTLE 244

Chapter 19
THE VALUE OF A TEN SHILLING NOTE 257

Chapter 20
INTROIBO AD ALTARE DEI
(I'LL GO UP TO THE ALTAR OF GOD) 268

Chapter 21
THE FADING GLOW...286

THE CORNCRAKE'S CALL 298

INTRODUCTION

My childish view of the world consisted of two very different landscapes, which were firmly fixed in my mind. One was made up of the lanes and hills and valleys and streams around the big fort, which dominated the hill of Sessiagh, my native townland. It was the place where I spent my childhood days with my friend and constant companion, Tommy Jordan. Tommy was the son of our next-door neighbours, and like me, he was an only child.

The long days of summer were spent scourging hoops, or playing games, or fishing in the streams for sprickleys. In winter there were lots of places to slide, often enjoying great craic having snow fights, and we could sledge down the fort hill till our hearts content. We could also slip down to the lough when no one was looking. The lough was like a great sea to us, and quite often we played dangerous games along its shores. That landscape was real for in it, and amongst its people, I had the good luck to be born and reared.

The other place I knew well was the centre of the great city of Glasgow. In the days of my infancy, my mother kept telling me of the wonderland where she had spent her youth. So used was I to listening to her voice, that when I went to school I had a clearly defined Scottish accent, and adults used to encourage me to talk, in order to hear, 'the wee Scotch fellow from Sessiagh.' I would wander down Argyle Street and look at all the wonderful things in the shop windows, or marvel at the way the whole place was glittering in the electric lights, even in the long dark nights of winter. I could only imagine such a scene because I had never seen electric lights in reality. Or I would stroll through the Glasgow Green, which was an endless and beautiful park, near to my mother's home, and a place where you could meet people from all over the world.

I would spend time too round the wonderful stalls in the market, which was just across the London Road from the big house where my mother had been reared. I would even take a boat down the Clyde and call at Greenock where my mother's people had a clothes shop, or go to the Kyles of Bute for my holidays, and visit Fingal's cave, and see the statue of Our Lord which had some sort of other- world property. I knew that taking such a trip was known as 'going doon the water for the fair.' This landscape had been etched in my mind by my mother's constant descriptions of the totally delightful place she had left, to come 'to this God-forsaken land.'

At the same time I could not help hearing the news from the neighbours, who came to the house at night, and I was somewhat thankful that I did not have to keep dodging the big bombs, which Hitler's men were so intent on dropping on the city. Like my mother, I was concerned for the safety of my aunts and uncle, whom I had never seen, but whom I had come to know as very superior beings. They were definitely gifted with minds of a quality, which the people around my native place could not even imagine. They were not stupid nor ignorant nor uneducated, like the country people amongst whom my mother had settled. It was a rich

The Glow of the Oil Lamp

and wonderful world, untouched by the glow of the oil lamp.

Benburb school building has changed very little in sixty years though the pupil numbers have fallen markedly. The two storeyed part was the headmaster's living quarters.

CHAPTER 1
I GO FORTH, BLINDLY

I was one month over six years old when they sent me to school. I had been fortunate enough to enjoy an extra year of glorious freedom at home. This piece of luck was due in no small measure to the fact that my mother believed that, being a Dawley, I would be brainless. She had given me the impression that the idea was clearly fixed in her mind, that because of this unfortunate genetic fact, starting school a year late, would make no difference at all. Much later I would realise that her words probably reflected the city born person's view of country life and country people. The child, however, absorbs what he hears and this can have an impact on his mind, which the parent never intended.

My first day at school turned out to be a strange and somewhat traumatic experience. It was not because I had to walk a mile to the village, nor even because I believed that I would never keep up with the other children, which made going to school seem to me a worthless and foolish exercise, nor even because I felt very shy in meeting people. But I was a lone Catholic sent unarmed and unwarned, into totally Protestant territory.

Nobody had bothered to explain to me what this meant, which probably would not have been possible anyway. I had no idea at all that for a young Catholic to venture into a Protestant school, was somewhat akin to a young lemming gambolling ignorantly towards the steepest cliff in the land. The precariousness of my new position was brought home to me rather forcefully at break time, on my first morning, in the school playground.

Near the entrance to the playground stood the remains of a huge old tree, which had been cut at a height of four feet or so. It was the sole piece of plant life to have survived anywhere in the tarmac surfaced yard. I found myself corralled at this tree-stump, surrounded by hordes of huge boys and girls. At least that is how they appeared to me, for I had never encountered a crowd of children before. They were all eager to see and examine this 'wee fenian', and convey the message that 'Papishes' were not welcome in their domain.

I had not the slightest notion what they were talking and yelling about, but I knew that I was an alien. I sensed that I was in imminent danger and that for some reason this mob hated me. I wondered if they realised that I was stupid and would not fit in with school life. I wondered too, if I would survive my first morning, never mind the horrible years that I had convinced myself lay ahead. The slow banter about Taigs and Fenians and Papishes changed to a fanatical chant:

The Glow of the Oil Lamp

Green, white and yella is a dirty wee fella
Red, white and blue is both loyal and true.

I had not the remotest notion as to the significance of these colours, but I realised that for some reason I was a dirty wee fellow. I was pushed and pummelled from one senior boy to another, like some hateful and pitiful plaything. Finally one big boy stepped from the crowd, grabbed me by the hair, and with all his force, bashed my forehead into the bark of the old tree. Blood streamed down my forehead and into my eyes. Blood and tears streamed down my face and on to my jersey. The crowd faded into a mist and I thought I must be dying.

My next memory is of a huge fat man standing over me, and venting his anger on the crowd around the tree-stump. I knew that he was Mr. Howard, the headmaster, for I had seen him when my mother took me on a visit to the school a few days before. Then he sat behind a great wooden desk, looking big and powerful. His great red face and deep polished voice had filled me with awe. But now that voice was soft and soothing as he spoke to me in a friendly whisper. "Are you all right child? What have they done to you at all, at all? I'll have the hide of a few fine boys for this. What sort of savages would do the likes of this? June, go and get a towel from the house." The voice remained very soft and gentle, soothing and yet angry. But I sensed that the anger was not directed at me. The big hands that held my shoulders were kind and gentle too. I felt that this big man whom I had dreaded so much, was my friend and saviour. His final words had been addressed to his daughter. Soon she came out of their house, which was attached to the school, carrying a towel.

June was a senior pupil at the time and she wrapped the towel round my neck and gently led me into the house. Here, at a sink, which was an item I had never seen before, she washed my face and bathed my wound. After a minute or so, she was joined by her mother, who was also my teacher. "Look what they have done to the poor wee innocent fellow, Mammy," she said, "If Daddy hadn't stopped them they'd have half killed him. I really thought, Mammy, that they were going to do him a serious injury. I ran for Daddy as soon as I saw what they were at."

Mrs Howard and June dressed and bandaged my wound and then insisted that I take a cup of tea. June was given the job of seeing that no serious harm came to me for the rest of the year. It wasn't that she had to spend much of her time with me, but she had to keep and eye on me, so that I could not be lynched.

June was a wonderful and kindly girl. She not only saved me from the hostile mob on that first morning but in the following months she helped me with my tables and spelling, and slowly convinced me that I was not as stupid as I had thought. Soon I got to know my classmates and they became my lifelong friends. June's kindness overwhelmed me and with the new confidence she gave me, I began to look forward to going to school most days. I had fallen in love for the first time, and maybe six is not too bad an age to do that.

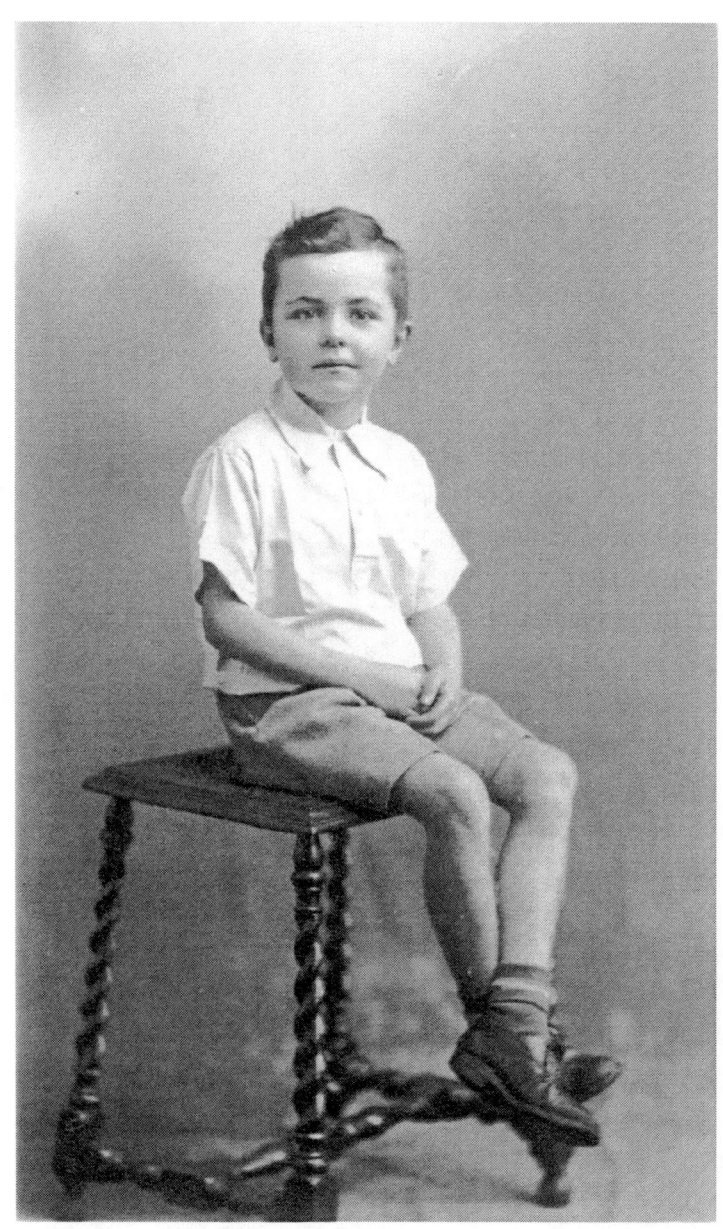

Reluctant to go to school after an extra year of freedom to explore and enjoy the wide green fields of Sessiagh

CHAPTER 2.
SESSIAGH : A TOWNLAND LIKE NO OTHER

Situated about a mile from the school in Benburb, my native townland of Sessiagh would seem extremely isolated and remote to a stranger used to city or even village life. In my earliest years it took quite a long time to get even to the tiny village of Benburb, for everyone had to walk or go by horse and cart. For those who could afford a bicycle, the gravelled road into the townland was so rough and dotted with potholes, that this fairly novel method of transport was not a very comfortable alternative. For some reason, which I still do not understand, people who rode bicycles always seemed to be getting punctures, so that these machines spent as much of their lives up-side-down as they did carrying their owner. And the younger that owner was, the more prone he seemed to accumulate punctures.

At the heart of our townland is a hill topped by a huge ring-fort, from which one can view most of the counties of Tyrone and Armagh. Parts of Antrim and Down are visible too in the farther distance to the east, whilst to the south west the hills of Monaghan can be seen as well. There is no doubt that the tribesmen who built the great fort some thirteen hundred years ago, chose a spot from which one could view everything worthwhile, which was happening in large parts of five counties. One also has a much closer view of the whole sweep of the river Blackwater, almost from its source until it reaches Lough Neagh. But the thing that attracted my friend Tommy and I, most of all as children, was the massive surrounding moat of the fort, some fifteen yards wide and in most places twenty feet deep. It was certainly a magical playground for us, and a place where imagination could run wild.

The great ring fort of Sessiagh is the centrepiece of a large fortified area. To the south of it, and about half a mile distant, on a lower hill, is Lisduff, which means the black fort. To the north, also about half a mile away is the small, but well preserved fort of Lisgobban. Gobban was the mythical builder of Irish legend, and is credited with the construction of all sorts of wonderful castles, forts and houses in prehistoric times. In between these two, to the west are, Lisnacroy, which means the fort of the gallows, and Lisbancearney, which means Kearney's white fort. Finally to the north east and almost a mile distant, is Lisbanleimaneigh, the white fort of the horse leap.

The strange thing is that all these outlying forts are small, indeed some are not even recognisable as forts nowadays at all, and yet they have given names to the townlands in which they are situated. Sessiagh or Sessiamagaroll, however, encompasses the biggest and clearly the most important fort of all, and yet the townland name makes no reference to it. Sessiagh in the

Irish is a sixth, but there is still a lot of debate amongst academics as to what the rest of the name means. One of the latest theories is that it may be MacFhearghaill, referring to the sons of Fergal, who was a king, killed in battle in the seventh century. It is even suggested that it was Fergal who had the fort built.

To the west of Sessiagh fort and some five hundred yards away in a deep valley is Curran Lough. It takes its name from a small townland, which touches the water's edge at its northern end, but only for some fifty yards or so. Other townlands have a much greater length of boundary and in fact it is sometimes referred to as Sessiagh Lough by the locals, because our townland takes up a big section of the circumference. This oval of water, exactly one mile in circumference had a magnetic attraction for us as children. And the thing, which was most alluring because it was out of reach was the island at its centre. At that time we did not know that it was a crannóg or man-made island, built on horizontal oak logs, and designed as the last refuge of the king in time of war. My father was always warning me never to go near the lough. It was far too dangerous. It was full of springs and whirlpools and even for the strongest swimmers it was a deathtrap. There was a widely held belief that every seven years this peaceful and beautiful place claimed a life.

My childhood was marked by one exceptionally severe winter, when ice was so thick on flaxholes that it could not be broken with a hammer. I had experienced its strength when sleighing down the hill, hitting a bank at the bottom, and landing on my head on the ice of

The Glow of the Oil Lamp

the flaxhole. The lough too was covered with thick ice, and apart from areas where the surface looked strangely black, it appeared both strong and safe. My father told me that the black areas showed where there were underwater springs. These created whirlpools and were very dangerous.

On an evening when our parents were busily engaged, Tommy and I made our way down to the water's edge. The ice seemed safe and the island luringly near. We stepped boldly onto the frozen surface and while there was some crackling, it was away at the far side of the lake, and seemed to have little connection with the fact that our weight was being borne by the ice. Carefully but steadily we made our way outward and soon we were within twenty yards of the island. My father had told me that the last landlord had planted fruit bushes and roses on this isolated place, and I was anxious to examine them for myself.

Suddenly there was a tremendous crackling sound all around us, and fractures began to spread like the splintering of glass. We had no idea how deep the water was beneath the surface and we were now terrified. The question was whether to go on or to go back to the shore. We decided to go on and together we took one more step. It was as though the ice did not exist. We found ourselves standing in ice-cold water but it was only up to our knees. Now I remembered that my father had told me that around the island the water was very shallow indeed, and that at one time the island had been much bigger, covering most of the shallow centre of the lake. When the land had been taken from the landlords, local farmers salvaged lots of the oak beams to roof sheds and barns. It was now only a few steps through the freezing shallow water to reach the shore. Our journey was a great disappointment. There was nothing to be seen on the island. The shore, which we had left, was a much more interesting place.

We were now faced with the problem of how to get back. The ice near the island was wafer thin as we could see where it had broken. We decided to wade out to where it was thicker, but the problem was how to reach ice, which would take our weight. We knew that the water would get deep very quickly and was deadly dangerous. By this time Tommy and I had changed schools, and Mr. Colgan our teacher, had given us a lesson on spreading weight. We knew that if we could spread our weight out well enough, we had a much better chance of success. The most dangerous thing to do was stand on one's two feet, for then all the weight was on a very small surface.

We got a pole on the island about eight feet long, and waded out to where the ice was still thick but cracked. Tommy lay face down and I pushed him out with the pole. I pushed him out as far as the pole would reach and the ice held, but it was crackling as though it were about to disintegrate under him at any moment. He managed to turn round to face me and when I lay down he tried to pull me towards him. But as I slid towards him, he also came sliding back towards me. Eventually we laid the pole on the ice, and while he held the end, I used it to ease myself outward. We were making very slow and dangerous progress. The now thunderous crackling of the ice warned us that our lives were hanging by a thread.

We decided to move as far apart a possible in order to spread the weight better. We put the pole between us so that each could reach it with one hand. In this way we edged ourselves, inch by inch, towards safety. We were probably half way to the shore before we decided it might be safe to stand up. Tommy stood up and the crackling around the lough was unbelievable. He sat down again and now began to move backwards towards the shore on his backside, using his feet to push himself along. It was slow but better and I did the same. We managed to get within twenty yards of the shore and wondered if it would be safe to try standing up again. I began to rise but the crescendo of crackling was almost deafening. I remembered my father had said the bed of the lake was shallow for some feet from the shore, and then fell steeply. It was impossible to know when we had reached the shallow part. Darkness and freezing fog were now descending and panic began to grip us.

We turned on our tummies again and using the pole, continued our painfully slow progress towards our goal. But at least we were making progress. Suddenly we heard voices shouting our names in the distance. In the chill of the winter evening those voices echoed and re-echoed from the surrounding hills. We wondered if we should reply but decided to keep quiet for another few minutes. Now we were only seven or eight yards from safety. The ice was cracking dangerously and still we did not dare to stand up. Suddenly Tommy's father and my father, burst through the bushes at the water's edge, and stood on the spot we were aiming for.

"You can stand up all right now", said Tommy's father, "The ice will take your weight all right there. What the hell took the two of you out into that hole at this time of the evening? It's not as if you weren't told often enough about it. You are damned lucky to be alive. The two of you deserve to get the hide taken off you for doing such a foolish thing."

We stood up and stiffly walked to the shore, the ice cracking loudly under our feet. But it held. I thought the men would kill us, but they grabbed us and hugged us. They were so glad to get us back that our foolishness was forgotten. And we had learned a lesson that neither of us forgot for it nearly cost us our lives. Perhaps it is due to Mr. Colgan that it did not.

All around the great hill in my youth, were scattered the dozen small-fielded, high hedged farms, belonging to the families who lived within the confines of the townland. The thatched houses with their small windows and half-doors were joined by gravelled lanes which were very narrow, scarcely wider than a horse's cart. The houses were scattered, sometimes a couple of hundred yards apart, sometimes up to half a mile. Ours was different in that it was nearly touching Conlon's, but sitting at right-angles to it, so that each family had a lot of privacy. There were also well-trodden paths through the fields, which marked the shortcuts from one house to another, or routes taken by people when walking to town. The inner part of the fort, which crowned the townland, was a wood of huge oak and beech trees, which had been planted by a landlord over a hundred and fifty years beforehand.

This wood to me was a cool place of mystery and adventure, even on the hottest summer day. It was also a place of great beauty, not only from inside but for those looking at it from afar, and it was a landmark from which people took their bearings if they were away from home. Sadly the timber was requisitioned and cut down in the war years, and the place has ever since been like a shattered skeleton of itself.

From my earliest days I always knew that we were poor for my mother kept telling me so, and she always made sure that I knew that, "the poor make no new friends". It was a condition I thought we shared, for our neighbours used to feed a litter of wee pigs in a hole in the kitchen floor, which was a couple of feet in front of the fire and they were big farmers. But above all things I regretted that we had no horse, not only because a horse was a mark of status, but also because I loved horses. Quite often I had to help my mother wheel a bag of coal or meal in a big pram from the shop in Benburb. The lack of a horse in some respects slightly blighted an otherwise happy childhood, and emphasised the fact that whereas all the other men in the townland were farmers, my father was a labouring man.

CHAPTER 3
THE PRIDE OF HAVING A TIN ROOF

Almost every day at some time I would have to walk with my mother to Benburb. It was an outing that I enjoyed immensely for my mother would always spend the time telling me about the wonderful times she had spent along the banks of the Clyde in her beloved Scotland. The country road between Sessiagh and Benburb was lined with huge trees on each side, and I do not think there was ever a time when I did not marvel at its beauty. But from the comments my mother made about the houses we passed on our way, I was always aware that she was very proud of the fact that we had a tin roof on our house, at a time when all the others still had the thatch. I am not sure if it was because she had been reared in Glasgow, but she certainly saw this as a mark of status. She pointed out that thatch attracted rats and she hated rats. It also attracted birds, and in trying to find a place to make a nest, or in stealing material, these creatures caused lots of damage, and keeping the rain out was a constant heartbreak. She failed to remark that thatch was much warmer and cosier, or perhaps she did not realise that.

She often told me the story of how we came to have the tin roof. A few years before I was born, my mother's old aunt Bel, was reading in bed one night with a candle, when she fell asleep with the candle still lit. She awoke to find the bed and the room blazing, but managed to get outside without being hurt. But the house was burned entirely and it was said that the fire could be seen for miles.

The neighbours came from far and near to try to save what they could, which was not much. Barney Jordan, who lived only a few hundred yards away, told me years later, that Bel's main concern was for bags or boxes in which she had money, and which she had hidden above the door or up in the loft. People at that time did not trust their money to banks, partly because it was difficult to get to the town when one needed money quickly, but more importantly they saw bank officials as part of the governmental system. It was very bad policy to let strangers know one's business, especially if those strangers were in positions of power. And anyone who wore a shirt and tie and a suit to work was seen to be in a position of power. In Bel's case Barney managed to save one parcel from above the door, but the others were lost in the inferno.

My father was a young fellow at the time and was a trainee stone mason. He was also a distant relative of Bel's, so he was given the job of rebuilding the house. He lived only a couple of miles away, and so he was a natural choice for the job. He added a new bay to the repaired remains of the two bays already there, and he roofed the entire building with tin, or corrugated iron

The Glow of the Oil Lamp

as it is often called. It was while he was engaged in this job, that my mother came over from Glasgow where she had been born and reared. She came to live with her aunt Bel in the place where her father had been born, because she had a chest infection, and the doctor advised her to go and live somewhere where there would be plenty of fresh air. Certainly, if there was little else in Sessiagh at that time, there was plenty of fresh air. My father took such a fancy to the 'wee Scotch lassie' that he never left the house until the day he died nearly sixty years later. And he maintained that he never managed to get the job completely finished either, for every time he made some improvement, my mother had another job waiting for him to start.

    I don't really remember the old aunt, for she died when I was less than three years old, but my parents used to tell me how she would nurse me by the fire, and roast big bramley apples, in the greesiagh, for me to suck. She was known far and wide as auld Bel Bloomer, and she was a favourite with all who knew her. More than sixty years later people who knew her as children, remember her with affection, and recall how kindly and caring she was to all the children round about. She has also lingered in my imagination and I often find myself picturing her by the hob and the crane crook, in her long black dresses. It is certainly true that the night Bel's house went on fire became one of the landmarks by which people of the neighbourhood measured time. Until a few years ago it was common to hear people say, "that was a couple of years before Bel set the house on fire", or " that happened the year after Bel's house was burned to the ground."

Apart from my mother, Bel was the last of the Bloomer family to live in the little farm where I was born. Her people used to 'own' nearly all the land in some five townlands around ours, but they had slowly declined in importance, wealth and power over many years. While it was said that people 'owned' land, they in fact rented it, and they remained there much at the whim of the landlord or his agent, especially if they were Catholics. In some fashion I think my mother inherited her fear of poverty from the ancestral dread of not being able to pay the rent, which led to eviction.

Old Bel told my father how the Bloomers had come to Sessiagh for the first time. She warned him, however, not to tell anyone about it because, "they came with William of Orange and you would not want the people blethering and gabbling about the likes of that."

"Before he came to Ireland, and even before he came to England", she said, "William had a kingdom in France. At that time there were very few Protestant people in France, but those who were Protestant, looked to William for protection. But he had also many Catholics who were loyal to him, and amongst them was a man called William Bloomer. This man joined William's army and became a sergeant in the Dutch Blue Guards. This force was the king's bodyguard, the elite of all his troops, and they were all Catholics. Before very long, young Bloomer found himself invading England and eventually Ireland."

"Soon after he came to Ireland, he was sent with his friend Francois Du Cambon to attack the fort at Charlemont. After the capture of the fort, he went on with the rest of the army to fight at the battle of the Boyne. He survived the battle, and he returned to our part of the country. He married a girl he had met while taking part in the siege at Charlemont, and they were given a lease of land near Benburb, and centred on the townland of Sessiagh. At first things went well, but down through the ages the agents of the landlord managed to take the Bloomer land from them through trickery. They were greatly helped by the fact that many of the Bloomers, in successive generations, were far too fond of the drink."

Bel had hoped that her brother Arthur, my mother's father, would stay on the place and extend it and make a good farm of it, but bad times came and he was working as a young man of sixteen for sixpence a week. When he got the chance he made his way to Scotland, and eventually to Glasgow, where he married a girl from the Donaghmore area, called Alice Creggan. My mother was the only member of their family of nine to return to the old homestead.

It was the hungry thirties in those days following my parents' marriage, and my father found it hard to get any sort of work. It was a bit of a blow when old Bel died, not only because she was greatly loved, but she had the old age pension of five shillings a week, and that was a sore loss when there was nothing else coming in. I remember my mother telling me how she had spent a whole week's money, buying my father a pair of working boots, and how he took the soles off them in the following week, when he was cleaning out sheughs for a farmer, at the rate of a shilling a day. It seemed to me that in some way she never quite forgave him, and that she got it into her head that to some extent he did it on purpose.

It so happened that some years later when I was seven or so, a Jewish man came to live in a house across the fields from us. He was always trading in one thing or another, and at a time when there was no chance of getting things without coupons, and there was no chance of getting coupons, he could supply anything anyone wanted for the right price. And that price was always very high indeed.

My mother went across the fields to the Jew's house, and bought some clothes. She took a great delight in being part of the trade, for it reminded her of how she had worked in her family's clothes shop in Greenock. I remember having to wait in one room, in much the same way as one had to wait to get into the doctor's surgery. Finally we were allowed into the inner room, where shelves were lined with all manner of clothes and other articles, so that the place seemed to me like an Aladdin's cave. I think it had the same effect on my mother, and I am sure she would have been happy to stay there all night. But the Jew had a roomful of customers waiting, and he was not interested in hearing how the trade was carried on in Scotland. One of the things my mother bought was a pair of working trousers for my father, a pair of the very best moleskins she said.

The Glow of the Oil Lamp

The following Saturday my father was going off to the hunt as usual. He was throwing his leg over the barbed wire fence in our front field, when the cloth caught on one of the barbs and he ripped the leg of the new trousers from top to bottom. He said that the blooming trousers were pure rotten, and that the mole had been quare and lucky to get rid of such rotten skin. He advised her to bring them back to the bloody Jew where she got them, but she just shook her head sadly and said, "it's like I said, the Dawleys are just plain stupid. He did the very same thing with the new boots. I don't know how I'm expected to keep him clothed. He's going to end up wearing a barrel and a pair of wellingtons."

In my very early years, a big problem for us and for our neighbours, the Conlons, was the fact that neither of us had a spring well of our own. In those days there was no piped water nearer than the village, and no one could have foreseen the day when it would come to a backward place like our townland. There was a general belief that pipe water was bound to be bad for people anyway, whereas good spring water was one of the healthiest things that man could drink. Since we had no well my mother had to carry water from a spring at the bottom of Jordan's meadow. I gathered from her attitude that she thought the neighbours were not too happy about her taking the water at all. This is most unlikely, since they had a well at the side of their house. She used to take me along with her, as she carried the two big white enamelled buckets. We walked up our lane for about two hundred yards, and entered the meadow at a gap, which was at the edge of our land.

It was then about three hundred yards to the spring, which was at the very bottom of the field.

My mother was tiny and was never very strong, so she had to carry the buckets only partially filled. Even when my father made her a hoop from an old bicycle wheel, which kept the buckets away from her body, it was still a very long carry with many stops. My attempts to help must only have made the labour a lot more difficult for her. Usually of course, my father would leave water in the house before he went to work, but sometimes he was away so early that it fell to us to fetch it.

One day when I was about three or perhaps four, a man called Jemmy McCrory came to the house carrying a forked hazel stick. After sitting talking for a long time and drinking numerous cups of tea, he and my father went outside. Jemmy marched all around the house holding the forks of the stick so that the point stuck out in front of him about chest high. Every so often Jemmy would stop to give everyone a lecture on the numerous wells that he had found for people all around the countryside. My father agreed that he was the best well deviner in our part of the country. Suddenly, round at the back of the house, and just beside Conlon's barn, the stick nearly jumped out of his hands, and the point turned sharply downwards. To judge by the tension on his face, Jemmy appeared to use all his strength to hold it level, but it bent downwards in spite of him.

"There is a powerful strong spring there, Mick," said Jemmy, looking at my father with a big crooked smile on his face. "If you dig here, Mick, you will come on the water before you get to twenty feet." Jemmy then

The Glow of the Oil Lamp

took a pointed stick out of his pocket and drove it into the ground with a stone, explaining to my father that spot should be the exact centre for the well. Jemmy would not take any money for his work but apparently my father would owe him a good drink next time they met in the Moy. And it could take a whole day to supply Jemmy with what he considered a good drink.

The next day my father started digging, and for a while he drew the soil away in a barrow and put it in the front field. When he got down to about five feet, it got very difficult to shovel the soil into the barrow, and he had to have a ladder to get in and out of the hole. Soon the hole was so deep that he had to carry the soil up the ladder in a bucket, and empty each bucketful into the barrow. It was tedious and very heavy work, and after the third day he was so far down, that it was no longer possible. Or at least it was so slow and tiresome, that he said he would have to find some other way of getting rid of the soil.

At that point he made a thing he called a windlass, and explained to me that it was a wonderful machine. He said it had been used for thousands of years and that it was still as efficient as ever. It consisted of two strong wooden posts on each side of the well, with a strong beam joining them. Across these beams, and traversing the centre of the well, was a wooden log, about four feet long, with metal axels at each end, where it rested on the beam. These were held in place with steel pegs so that the log could turn but could not roll off. To one side of the log he fitted a big handle like the starting handle of a car. With this my mother could easily turn the log. To the log he then attached a strong rope, which was much longer than would reach to the bottom of the well. This was wound round the log so that my mother could lower the bucket down to my father in the well. Apart from anything else it meant that it was much easier to work in the well without the ladder.

From that point on my father stayed down in the hole, and each time he filled the bucket with soil he shouted, "Right Sarah," to my mother, and she turned the handle so that the bucket was raised to the top. When my mother told me to do so, I had to put a wooden peg into a hole, so that the handle would not spin backwards, when she got it to the top and let go of it. She then unhooked the bucket, emptied it into the barrow and lowered it into the hole again.

It was slow work and must have been very heavy for a little woman like my mother, for she had to pull the bucket towards her, before she could get a grip on it, in order to take it and empty it. She said that she had read in books about slaves who worked in the mines, but she never thought that she would come to Sessiagh to do the same kind of work. I cannot recall how long the job took, but at seventeen feet my father struck water, and he had to get the ladder lowered, and get out quickly, because the water was rising quickly. That was a tricky enough operation, for by that time my mother had to use the windlass in order to lower the ladder to him. It was a great advantage to have a spring well at the back of the house, and in the years that followed I drank gallons of its water for it was both cool and delicious.

The Glow of the Oil Lamp

The sinking of the well did not pass without one incident, which I will never forget. My father was down in the well one day, at about fifteen or sixteen feet I think. My mother had to go into the house for something. For some reason that I cannot explain, I decided to see how deep the well was by throwing a stone down. I picked a lovely pebble about the size of a golf ball and fired it down as hard as I could. It bounced off the top of my father's head. Fortunately for me he could not get out until my mother lowered the ladder, by which time I was hidden under the bed. From the threats and curses that he uttered and which I could hear clearly, even in the house, I reckoned I was lucky to see the completion of the evening, never mind the completion of the new spring well. Years afterwards he would claim to be the only man in the country, who had a son who had attempted to eliminate him, but he said he had read about some old boy in the bible, who had had the same experience.

Curran Lough with its crannóg viewed from its eastern shore. It was believed that the lake claimed a life every seven years.

CHAPTER 4
BESSIE THE GOAT AND TRIMMER THE DOG

The goat arrived in the very early part of the year in which I started school. My father told me one lovely spring morning to go and see if there were any eggs in the shed at the top of the street, which was next to the byre. I thought this a strange order for my mother knew exactly where the hens laid, and she liked to collect the eggs herself. Furthermore she had collected the eggs late on the previous evening, and early morning was never a time for looking for eggs anyway. However, I set off to do as I was told.

I went in through the byre and climbed over the wooden railing that divided the byre from the calves' shed. I had looked in all the usual places, and was just about to give up, when I looked over a wooden rail in the corner. I did not see any eggs but lying there in a neat bed of straw, was the loveliest little white animal I had ever seen. At first I thought it was a pup, but having climbed over the railing, I realised it was a kid goat. I lay down on the straw beside it and it snuggled into my arms. I lay there stroking and petting it, and the more I did so the more it nuzzled up against me. I do not think

I ever felt as close to any living thing, and I fell in love with it at once, and I still believe it fell in love with me.

"Come on in and get your tea, son, and don't spend all day there with that kid." It was my mother who was standing smiling in the shed, and looking down at me. Reluctantly I laid down the kid, and went with my mother into the house. "Well, what do you think of your new friend?" asked my father. "You have been cleaning out the byre for the cows well, so I hope you will be able to look after it."

"Is it mine Da? Did you get it for me? Where did you get it? What will I give it to eat?"

"Och dammit, if I thought we were going to have all these questions, I think I'd have left it where it was," said my father with a sly look and a wink at my mother.

"But where did you get it Da?"

"I got it yesterday from a man when I was away at the hunt. He lives away up at the far side of the county Monaghan. I told him that I knew a wee fellow who would be able to look after it, and take good care of it."

"What does it need to eat Da? I'd better go and feed it now."

"Take your tea first. The wee kid won't starve. You'll have to give it milk from the cow for a while, but after that it will almost be able to look after itself. When I was a wee lad your age we had a goat at home, and we called her Bessie."

"Well, Da I think we'll call this goat Bessie as well." For some reason that I did not understand, Da nodded his head in agreement, and it was clear that he was very well pleased indeed.

In the months that followed I lay with the kid in its bed at times, and for most of the day it went everywhere with me like a dog. I slipped it into the house when my mother was not watching, and I even managed to slip it into the bed through the window for a while, until my mother found out. "Your Da's dafter than your are with that goat," she scolded. "I have a good notion to get him to take it back to where he got it. If I ever get it in your bed again it's definitely for the road."

All that summer my life revolved around my friend and companion the goat. I did not notice how big she had become, but for a while my parents were a little concerned for she was so big and strong, that they were afraid she would hurt me. I remember one night when I had persuaded my mother to let me bring her in to the house, and she and I were lying under the table. "You know, Mick," said my mother, "You know the way we were talking about the size of the goat the other day. Well I was at the door yesterday, and a cart was coming down the lane, and the wee fellow was in the lane. You would hardly believe it, but the goat pushed him into the hedge, and would not let him out till the cart had passed."

"Och, now Sarah," said my father with a big laugh, "Didn't I always tell you that half the people in the country are not nearly as clever as goats?"

"Well, anyway," replied my mother, "Nothing will happen to the child as long as that goat is about."

The summer was over and I had to go to school. The goat left me to the end of our lane each morning, and then she stayed grazing with the cattle in the fields until I came home. But as soon as I came down the lane, she got out of the field and came into the house, and stood beside me at the table while I took my dinner. The fact that we had a big white goat in the house every evening, greatly annoyed my mother. She pestered my father so that he fenced the fields time after time, but still the goat got out and rammed the door with her head, until she got into the house. "Be God," said my father, "I have fenced animals all my life, but the devil the likes of that goat ever I saw. The very devil himself could not keep her in, when that lad is about. When he's at school she'll stay in the field with no fence at all. I do believe that you could not get her to leave the cattle if you tried. But when the lad comes down the lane the whole of the bloody British army wouldn't stop her."

One evening, after a few months, I came home, and for some reason angered my mother. She gave me an awful scolding and also a few whacks with a stick. She took no notice of the goat standing at the side of the table. My mother went over to the fireplace to get something for the dinner. The goat charged, hit her full belt on the bottom with her head, and drove the poor woman half way up the chimney. I managed to help my mother down out of the second draught, covered in soot and sparks, but really not that much the worse for wear, except for the shock.

That weekend I went out on Saturday morning to play with my friend the goat. She was not in the field so

I looked in the shed. She was not there, so I searched all round the house. I searched all round Conlon's and Jordan's, but my goat was nowhere to be seen. My father was going to the hunt and I met him in the lane, crying my heart out. "Da, I can't find Bessie. Do you think some stranger might have stolen my goat? Or would she be caught in some of the sheughs? Da, give me a hand to look for her before you go to the hunt."

My father put his arm around my shoulder. He knelt down and looked into my eyes. "Look son," he said. "That goat nearly killed Mammy the other day. She's got too big and dangerous. I gave her away to old Lizzie Kerr; I'll get you a pup."

I went absolutely crazy, or as my father said later, "the lad went clean off in the head." I tried to kick him but he held me off. I tried to throw stones at him but he grabbed me and threw me over his shoulder. He carried me to the house and made me lie down on the sofa. I didn't speak to my mother for a week. I tried not to speak to my father either, but he managed to make that difficult. Gradually the pain and loss eased, but I do not know if I ever really forgave them for taking my goat. One night, some time later, I heard them talking to each other about how Bessie had nearly killed old Lizzie, by pulling her up and down the steep banks of the Blackwater at Benburb. In my heart I think I wished she had succeeded and come home to me. But that was not to be.

Not long after the disappearance of my goat, my father brought home Trimmer. When Trimmer first arrived at our house he was a tiny pup, tan and black and white in colour. He was a hound or harrier, a breed of dog that is used for hunting the hare. My father had been an addict of this sport since his earliest days, and would proudly announce, "Everybody knows that Mick Dawley of Sessiagh is the best huntsman in the country."

The aim of the sport is not to catch nor kill the hare, but to own the dog, which is best at following the scent, chasing the hare, or following her to her lair from a place at which she has fed. This last attribute is called feed hunting. My father claimed to have had some of the best dogs ever seen in the valley of the Blackwater, and indeed his fellow huntsmen swear to the truth of this statement to the present day. The men follow the dogs on foot, and have no interest at all in those who hunt from horseback, which is seen as a rich man's sport.

For a short time I did not bother with the pup, because I thought that it was some sort of attempt to salve their consciences for taking away my goat. But the little pup followed me everywhere, and at night would lie nowhere only at my feet. My father paid no attention apparently, and talked only of the day when this pup of his would be a great hunting dog. And I noticed that my mother went out of her way to talk only of Mick's dog. In no way did they indicate that they thought I should have anything to do with it.

Trimmer grew into a fine big dog and was the best of the pack, so that my father was the focus of attention when huntsmen visited their friends and rivals many miles away. I was proud of the stories I heard of his exploits, but I was prouder still of the fact that, if he had a chance at all, he would walk beside me, and at night was not happy unless lying across my feet at the fire. I knew in my heart that he would give his life, rather than let anyone or anything hurt me. The other thing that Trimmer did was accompany my mother to Benburb, when she went for her messages. Many a time she locked him up securely in a shed, only to have him overtake her half way to the village. On one occasion this led to a famous incident.

My mother had a friend called Maggie Donnelly, who was much younger than she was, and who was getting married. She lived in the village, and she brought my mother into the house to see all the dresses and things that she had for the wedding. In pride of place in the bedroom was the wedding cake, set out in three separate pieces. Having discussed all the various items as women do, Maggie and my mother went up to the kitchen, where Maggie insisted on having a cup of tea. Trimmer was left out on the street, and when my mother came out to finish her shopping and go home, she was surprised, for the dog was nowhere to be seen.

My mother came home to find Trimmer proudly standing guard over the top layer of Maggie's wedding cake, on the doorstep of our house. Although he had put his two front paws right through it, he had not eaten one iota. My mother was highly embarrassed and she did not know what to do. When my father came home that evening she hardly let him sit down before she blurted out, "Oh God, Mick, what should we do at all? Should I tell Maggie that our dog took the cake and brought it home? Or do you think I should keep my mouth shut, and hope that no one tumbles to the idea that our dog stole it?"

My father gave a howl of laughter and he rolled in the chair laughing.

"God Mick, it's no laughing matter. Poor Maggie needs the cake for the wedding is in a fortnight. What am I going to do at all? That bloody dog would eat anybody that touched a thing about this house, but he'd carry home all he sees belonging to other people."

My father looked at her, still laughing. "Och dammit, Sarah, I can't help seeing the funny side of how the dog brought home the wedding cake. You should have sent him back, and told him to fetch the other two pieces." Here he went into howls of laughter at his own joke. After a couple of minutes he settled down, pulled her onto his knee and looked up at her. "I tell you what we should do Sarah. You'd be giving Maggie a present anyway. Well give her a better one to make up for the loss of the cake, but never let on that the dog ever touched it."

The disappearance of the wedding cake was the talk of the village for weeks. All sorts of people got the blame, from Jack McGuigan who was always playing tricks on people, to small children, who could be forgiven since they did not know what they were doing. But it puzzled people that no trace of the cake was ever found, and all those who fell under suspicion denied having anything to do with it. But on my mother's next visit to Benburb, Maggie eyed Trimmer and asked, "There wouldn't be any chance that that dog took the cake, Sarah? I wouldn't like to chance that boy. It disappeared just about the time that you and me were taking the cup of tea. That's a powerful present you've given me. Now I didn't expect the likes of that."

My mother pretended hurt dignity. "Och Lord, Maggie, that dog would not touch a thing. I can leave the dinner on the table, and him in the house, and go out and he would not go near the table." In saying this, my mother had not told one word of a lie, and Maggie agreed that this was a good point, and the dog was obviously very faithful, but she still looked at him suspiciously, and my mother knew that she was not convinced. But the riddle of the cake was never solved.

One day my mother took me with her to Armagh where she had to do some special shopping. We walked to Benburb and got the bus, which went once a week. We left my father at home, cutting a hedge, and cleaning out a sheugh at the furthest point of our land. When we came home we were more than surprised to find the kitchen filled with all sorts of tinware, from pint tins to big tin bath-like containers with handles, which were supposed to be for holding milk. When my father came in and sat down on his chair by the fire, my mother looked at him and asked, "Under God, Mick, have you gone off the in head altogether? What under heaven made you buy all this stuff? We'll never find a use for the half of it. We might as well give it to the neighbours. You must have an awful pile of money that I know nothing about, when you can afford to throw it away like this. What came over you anyway?"

My father looked rather sheepish, and gave a nervous laugh. "Och dammit, Sarah, I had to buy it. I was away down at the drain, and I heard the dog going mad, barking and howling. I didn't bother for a while, but he kept at it, and I came up to see what was annoying him. He had a gipsy woman penned in the corner at the top shed, and he was jumping up and barking and she was scared to death. And the thing was she was about to have a youngster. I took all the stuff off her to get rid of her in case she would have it here in the house."

My mother looked at my father; she looked at the kitchen full of tinware; she looked at Trimmer lying at my feet, and then she sat down, pointed at my father and started to laugh. In all my life I never saw her laugh so heartily, and she could not stop and the tears ran down her face. Finally she did ease off enough to be able to speak and she looked up at my father now standing in the middle of the floor, and looking entirely foolish. "I suppose," she said, looking up at him with a knowing smile, "You'll be telling the huntsmen that Mick Dawley is the best midwife in the country, and he gets Trimmer to help him."

My father looked at her. He lifted the largest of the tin vessels, and stomping out to the door, he fired it as far as he could out over the garden hedge. Again my mother went into howls of laughter, the reason for which I could not fully fathom. And that night, before I went to sleep, I could hear her peals of laughter from time to time.

Barney Conlon had a sick sow. He got an old hen and killed her to boil for the sow, for that was supposed to be a great cure. He boiled her in a big pot on top of an American stove, which he had installed in place of

The Glow of the Oil Lamp

the open fire. My father was helping him and so was I, and we put coal and sticks in the stove, so that after a while the metal was white hot, and the water was plumping in the pot. It was a summer day and we left the hen boiling, while we went outside and sat down at the hayshed for a chat. After half an hour or so, we went in to get the hen. The pot was still plumping, the metal was still white hot, but there was no hen in the pot.

"Well, hell to the likes of that ever I've seen," said Barney. "How in hell's blazes could that hen have got out of the pot? Nothing in this world could take a hen out of that pot only the devil, and he would have had a job to do that himself." There was a long investigation as to what might have happened to the hen. But there was no logical answer. We gave up and went outside. On the far side of the street Trimmer was lying with the hen between his paws, and looking very proud of himself. Barney looked at him. "Well how the hell you took that hen out of that pot I'll never know," he said, and went over to lift her. The dog stood up and bared his teeth, and the hair stood up on the back of his neck. "Be God," said Barney, " You took the hen out of the pot, and there's nobody going to take her off you. To hell with you and her, you deserve her so you can keep her." Barney backed off and Trimmer lay down over his hen peacefully.

"Hi Boy," my father said to me, "Go and get that hen for Barney's sow."

Barney nearly had a fit. "What the hell do you mean sending the child near that wild animal," he shouted. "There's not a man in Ireland could take that hen from

The Glow of the Oil Lamp

that dog without getting torn to pieces. And you send a child to do the job?"

My father did not reply but pointed to the hen. I walked over, patted the dog on the head, lifted the hen and handed her to Barney. Trimmer never moved a muscle except to wag his tail and lick my hand. Barney told the story to everyone he met for weeks to come. And how Trimmer managed to get the hen out of the pot was a subject of conversation in the houses all winter but no one ever solved the puzzle.

Trimmer was about three years old, and at the height of his powers, when my father took him one Saturday to a big hunt, which was at the Red Hills away in the county Cavan. Next morning the dog did not come to lick my face before I got up, and I jumped out of bed to look for him. He was nowhere about the house, and when I approached my father, he behaved in a guilty fashion, and explained that a lot of the dogs had not been caught on the previous evening.

On Sunday afternoon my father and I went round all the houses of the huntsmen, but none of them had brought Trimmer home, and none of them had heard any news of him. All of them complimented my father on the wonderful day's hunting the dog had done, and how he had made a fool of the Cavan dogs. But nobody had a clue as to what might have happened to him. I knew that big hunts ended with men getting quite a lot of drink, and I was not sure that my father had done a lot to find him. "Don't worry son, the dog will come home," he assured me. "That dog has more sense than most human beings. He'll be home before night." But my father's words rang hollow.

Trimmer did not appear that day nor on the following morning, though I must have got up twenty times during the night to look for him. I knew that my father was worried too when he said, "If he's not home by the weekend I'll go up to the Red Hills to look for him."

"I suppose you took as much care of him as you did of my goat," I growled.

My father looked at me. "Never as long as you live, talk to me like that again," he said. I could see anger mixed with disappointment and annoyance in his eyes. "You know well enough that I'd give my right hand for Trimmer. But he'll come home. You'll see." Trimmer did not come home that week, and on the following Saturday my father and a few of his friends went away to the Red Hills to look for him. They searched everywhere and asked all the men, who were huntsmen in that area, but there was no sign of him. When my father came home he simply shook his head, and I went off to bed with a sore heart.

The following week dragged slowly past, and it was a real pain to have to go to school for my mind was on the lost dog. When the next weekend came and went, and there was still no sign of him, everyone gave it up as a lost cause. He must have been shot or poisoned. I just could not settle. I wanted to know what had happened to him. I spent a fortune lighting candles to St. Anthony on my way to and from school. I prayed to everyone I could think of, and I asked everyone I met if they had heard any word of Trimmer.

Twenty six long and lonely days slowly passed. My father went out on his ceili to one of the neighbour's houses and my mother, who had a cold, went to bed early. The door was left on the latch for my father coming home. I went to bed at ten or so, but I tossed and tumbled and could not get to sleep. I must have drifted off in spite of myself, when I awoke to hear a slight whimpering, and feel a wet tongue licking my face. I jumped out of bed and threw my arms round the quivering bundle of mud and blood and dog, as he lay whimpering against me.

"Ma, Ma, Ma," I yelled, "Trimmer's back, Trimmer's back, come and see Ma, he's here with me." My mother appeared in her night clothes. She looked at the two of us, and there were tears in her eyes. "Oh God would you look at the state of him?" she said, kneeling down beside us. "Oh God almighty what has happened to him at all? God knows where the craytur has walked from. There's not a pick of skin left on his poor feet."

We got him a tin of milk and soaked some bread in it. He licked the milk slowly a couple of times, but he would not touch the bread. My mother got warm water and some soap, and we washed him carefully, and she bathed his sore feet and put some sort of ointment on them. "Och God, but he's only skin and bone," she sighed, "They have had him tied up somewhere, and he has had to eat through the rope. Look at the way his neck is all sores. And his poor gums are all red, where he has had to chew some sort of rope. The poor thing is so worn out, that he's not able to eat and he's starving."

The Glow of the Oil Lamp

My mother told Trimmer to go to bed, but he simply snuggled closer to me, and it was clear that he did not want to leave me. At that moment the door latch lifted, and my father entered the house. My mother shouted to him to come to my room. "Mick, Mick, Mick, the dog's back. He came to the wee fellow's room. Och God, Mick, he's half dead." My father looked at the scene from the door, and my mother asked him to put the dog in his bed. "Come on Trimmer boy, come to bed," he ordered.

Never before had the dog refused to do what my father told him. Usually he seemed to sense what he would be told to do, and did it almost by instinct. But now he hung his head, laid it on my chest, and looked at my father without moving. I think that was the only time in my life that I ever saw my father cry. But now there were big tears in his eyes and on his cheek, and he rubbed them away with his sleeve, and then came over and knelt down and rubbed the dog's head. With his other hand he rubbed my head as well. "God it's great to see him home," he said. "You can sleep in peace now boy, for you haven't slept right for nearly a month. And by the looks of it neither has he. Sarah get some sort of blanket, and let Trimmer sleep here the night. You can't separate the two of them when the dog's in this state."

They got an old blanket and put it on the floor at the side of my bed and settled the dog on it. I lay with my hand out of the bed so that it rested on his head. But when they went to bed, I took the bedclothes and moved down beside him, for I reckoned that he would not be fit to climb into my bed. I lay with my arms around him and the two of us fell asleep. My friend had come home to me and I was happy.

They found us there the next morning, and my mother was annoyed at me lying on the floor in the winter. My father put his hand on her shoulder and said gently, "no harm done, Sarah. The lad's lucky to have a dog like that, for you usually only find one of them in a lifetime, and that's only if you're very lucky. I'm just powerful glad to see the two of them together again. I don't think I'd have ever forgiven myself for taking him to the hunt, if he hadn't come home."

Trimmer lived till he was old. I know my father was right, for I still feel lucky ever to have shared a part of my life with him.

CHAPTER 5
A NEW BEGINNING

I think I was just over eight years old when they decided that I should change, and go to the Catholic school, which was three miles away in Blackwatertown. Remembering my initiation to my first school, it was a prospect that I was not looking forward to at all. In fact, I had settled down in the Benburb school, and had now no problem getting on with everyone. I don't know if this was simply because they had got used to me, or because I had been joined by about ten other Catholic children, most of them from the village itself. But this situation was truly to the annoyance of the parish clergy, who had berated my father when he had dared to send me to the Benburb school.

I can still remember clearly the priest coming to our house, and ordering my father to have me changed immediately to my own school. That was a big mistake for one did not order my father to do anything, if one was serious about having a positive outcome. He stuck his heels in, and told the priest that he would send his son to whatever school he damned well liked, and it was no business of any clergyman to tell him what to do, or how to rear his son. It seems as though my father's stand was the signal for the opening of a dam. Soon a number of other Catholic parents decided to send their sons and daughters to Benburb too, so that we became a small community within a community, and as time passed we were simply accepted, and no one took the slightest bit of notice of us. As far as I know their main reason for sending me to the new school was that they felt I was now old enough for the longer distance. There was certainly no problem with the teaching in Benburb. Maybe also my father felt he had made his point, and it was time to show that he was not totally unreasonable.

It so happened that I had a large slice of luck a couple of weeks before I changed schools. I was sitting in the second seat, at the front of the chapel one Sunday, when a boy beside me, whom I did not know, began to poke me. This developed into a mini fight during the Mass, became quite vicious, and in the end I got slightly the better of it. It was a bit of a shock when I found out that this boy was the hard man of my new class in Blackwatertown, and even boys in senior classes feared him, for he was totally fearless. But he spread the word that I had fought him in the chapel so that, not only did I gain a reputation as a hard man myself, but Sean and I became the best friends in the whole school.

Compared with the modern and well appointed school in Benburb, the new school was a very different and surprising place. Girls had a school of their own across the road for a start, so that we had practically no contact with them, which was at first strange to me. Instead of the neat rows of single desks in Benburb, the boys in the senior room sat in long benches, each of which held six or seven pupils. There were six of these benches, which accommodated the top two classes, and most of the time the master sat perched on the end of one of these benches at the back of the room. The other class in the room sat on forms along the wall beside the door. In the front corner of the room, and placed at an angle to its two adjacent walls, a huge coal fire blazed in an open grate, and it was the job of one of the senior boys to see that it was always well stoked. I found it a lot more homely than the central heating radiators that I had known in Benburb, but it was dirtier and quite dangerous.

The thing that surprised me most of all, was that many of the boys were barefoot. Indeed, I think when I first joined the school, I was one of only a handful of boys who wore shoes. I soon discovered that wearing shoes was looked upon as a cissy thing to do, and that many of the lads had hidden their shoes and socks in a hedge, to avoid being objects of scorn. Many, however, were just too poor to afford footwear of any kind. Unknown to my parents I developed the practice of hiding my footwear at the foot of the Sessiagh brae, and going the rest of the way barefoot, even in the colder weather.

Playtime in the field beside the school held another surprise. I could not believe my eyes when the boys picked two teams for a game of football, and instead of keeping the ball on the ground they picked it up and ran with it. Many were expert at running while tipping the ball from hand to toe, which they called solo running. I was told that this was called Gaelic, and I was ashamed of my total ignorance of it. I decided that since I was seen as a hard man, I would have to become expert at this new sport.

A football was a rare thing for any individual to have in those days, and no boy in the school owned one as far as I know. In fact every so often the master would hold a collection, and buy one for the school. I firmly believe that he got a very poor response, and ended up paying the most of it himself. Parents did not see playing football, or partaking in other pastimes, as very important. In my case I needed to practice at home, and since we could not afford a ball, I had to make one.

The first one was made from a piece of cloth stuffed with feathers, but it was dull and lifeless, and when it got wet it was almost impossible to play with. Someone told me that a pig's bladder was a good substitute. I went across the fields to O'Neill's house, and asked John if he could get me one. John killed most of the pigs around a large area, and he told me to call back in a week, and sure enough he had four fine bladders for me. But when I got home I discovered that they were very difficult to blow up, and when I managed to get them blown up they were too small anyway. But I still used them to practice around the haystacks and hen houses. It was enjoyable and I knew I was making progress.

In the following weeks and months, there were all sorts of inventions that my friend Tommy Jordan and I used, to practice our football skill, for he had changed schools at the same time as I had. I discovered a large piece of cloth that my mother called wrexine, which had been used to cover chairs. From it I cut numerous roughly circular shapes and by sewing these together, I managed to manufacture the outer case for a football, which was roughly spherical in shape. I then got a balloon, blew it up inside the case, and we had a reasonable football, even if it was a bit light. The one big drawback of course was that it was very easily punctured, and often we had to wait a week to afford a new balloon.

Master Colgan was a tall, middle aged, kindly man, who took a great interest in all his pupils. He was tough but fair, and since I had little difficulty in learning the ridiculously long answers from the old Maynooth catechism, I was seldom in trouble with him. One of his great loves was the art of parsing and analysis, and he would set me great, complicated sentences for my homework. These had to be broken up and set out in a special format, so that all their various parts were listed under the appropriate heading. I think it became a sort of game to see if he could catch me out, and for that reason I developed a natural ability in this technique. The more complicated the sentence was, the better I was pleased, whereas most of the other boys hated the very sight of the task, and there was a queue waiting each morning to copy my homework.

While I enjoyed my time at Blackwatertown, the confinement of school was sometimes tough on a young healthy lad from the wide green fields of Sessiagh.

In our last couple of years, my friend Sean and I engineered a scheme, which for a time, gave us the freedom we craved on a good summer afternoon. One of our friends in the class was a boy called Horace, who got into trouble one day, got a terrible beating from the master, and ran off into the hills around the school. Sean and I were given the job of chasing him, catching him, and bringing him back to school. We set out after lunchtime and could see him on a hillside, about a quarter of a mile away. Out of sight of the school we did not hurry, and by the time we managed to get back, everyone was leaving, the day's lessons over. The master gave Horace sweets, told him he was sorry for being so hard on him, and of course he gave us sweets too for a good job well done.

The next day we explained to Horace that it was not nice being penned in school on a lovely summer day. We made it clear to him that it would be very much to our liking if he would run off when we told him to, so that everyone could have an afternoon in the open air. We also explained to him in very direct language, that if he did not run hard enough or often enough, we would kill him stone dead. The retribution the master might exact would be nothing, compared with what he would suffer, should he deprive us of the chance to have some free time. The scheme worked excellently for weeks until the master caught on that Horace was not going of his own volition. The result was that Sean and I had to stay in for an extra half hour every evening to do extra sums, and to help the master to clean the school. Mr. Colgan explained to us that smart fellows usually meet fellows who are just as smart as they are.

The tree-lined road between Sessiagh and Benburb is very beautiful, especially in summer when the trees are in full foliage.

CHAPTER 6
A PLAGUE OF HENS AND TURKEYS

An experience, which I remember clearly from my very early days, is going to Dillons at Blackwatertown, for a setting of eggs to put under the big Rhode Island red hen, that had started clocking. It was a six mile journey, there and back, and my mother had to carry the setting of eggs on the way home, and make sure that none of them got cracked. While we were on the road with the eggs, she kept warning me to pray that there would be no thunder for the next month, for if thunder came while the eggs were under the hen, they would all go bad, and we would have no chickens, and that would be a very big loss. I was detailed to pray also, that the hen would make a good mother, that rats would not come and steal the eggs, and especially that a fox would not happen to come some night and take the hen and the eggs for his supper.

I was also ordered to pray for a big hit of pullets with few, if any roosters, for roosters were no use at all, at that time. And last year Julie Jordan had a great hit of lovely pullets, and it was all due to Tommy's prayers, and Tommy was younger that me. My mother outlined a seemingly unending line of saints, to whom I might speak on the subject, and she assured me that since I was young and innocent, and I suppose ignorant, my prayers were sure to be answered. They were, according to her, more powerful than the prayers of grown up people. These strange, other-world people reminded me of the ghosts who lived around the lough, and the fairies who lived in the fort, but since my mother did not mention these folk, I kept quiet about them, fearing that I might have to intercede with them as well.

When we reached our destination Mrs Dillon made us a cup of tea, and made us feel that it was a wonderful day for her because we had come to visit. In getting ready for the tea she took a chair out from the corner of the table by the window, in order to give me a seat by the fire. As we were in the middle of the tea, Jemmy, her husband came in, and was so busy talking to his visitors, that he went over to where the chair had been at the window, and proceeded to sit down without looking. He landed with a clatter on the floor and I can still see the shock and surprise on his face, which was all you could see of him above the table. "Ah be Jasus, I've landed on me arse," was all he said, and Mrs Dillon gave him the rounds of the kitchen for taking the holy name in vain, and him living beside the chapel. I got the rounds of the kitchen too from my mother for tittering and laughing at the sight of Jemmy looking over the table, and I got a lot worse later on for telling my father, "Be Jasus Jemmy Dillon landed on his arse on the floor in the corner, when we were taking the tea."

The Glow of the Oil Lamp

The trip for the eggs must have reminded my mother of a story her aunt Bel had told her, and she told me all about it on the way. Obviously it had happened many years previously, at a time when Bel went fairly often to the market in Armagh on a Tuesday, to sell whatever farm produce she had. It was a walk of fourteen or fifteen miles there and back, and in the summer it must have been not only tiring, but hot too. On one occasion Bel set out with two big laying hens in a large wicker basket. There's an old proverb in Gaelic which says that " a hen gets heavy over a long distance," so that by the time Bel reached Armagh, she looked pretty hot and worn out. A dealer on a cart looked at her, and then at the hens in the basket, and then he asked her, so that all could hear, "Well, Stirabout Face, and what would you be wanting for the two hens?" My mother would go into fits of laughing at this description of her aunt. She explained to me that stirabout was another name for porridge, and most country people liked porridge made from yellow meal. To her it encapsulated exactly, the appearance of countrywomen who were hard at work, engaged in slavish tasks. It was in complete contrast with the fine and refined features of the ladies from Glasgow who, according to her, never had to do any work at all.

My mother prided herself in the fact that, having been reared in the heart of a city, she had quickly learned to be as good a farmer as was to be found anywhere. Her farming consisted of helping to look after a couple of cows, rearing their calves, churning milk and making country butter, keeping a couple of hundred hens, and

The Glow of the Oil Lamp

in the autumn, a flock of turkeys. It seems to me that as far back as I can remember, hens became the bane of my life, for there was always some unpleasant job to be done where hens were concerned. To be fair the hens were not too bad really until someone, inspired by the very devil himself, discovered or invented the deep litter. This meant that the floors of old sheds, which used to be great play areas, were covered with peat to about the depth of a foot or so, and then the house was filled with young hens. In damp weather the floors got wet, and then they had to be dug every day with a graip. It was a job my mother reserved for me once I got to the age of eight or nine, and I hated it with all my heart. There was a horrible smell of ammonia, and no sooner had one dug a section, than the hens had it tramped back into baked mud again.

In the winter the hens had to have tilley lamps from about four o'clock until bedtime. I really hated and cursed whoever had invented the tilley lamp, almost as much as I hated and cursed the inventor of the deep litter itself. As soon as I came home from school, there was a row of tilleys that had to be filled with paraffin oil, and lighted. This process involved soaking a cloth like piece of material, which was held in a steel holder, in menthylated spirit. It was then clipped round the stem of the lamp and lighted until it warmed the central stem of the lamp and the mantle. If one was exceptionally lucky, once the lamp was pumped full of air and a screw was turned, it lighted.

But most evenings at least one lamp refused to light. It had to be taken apart and the vaporiser, which was inside its central stem, cleaned and checked. In order to do this one had to carefully remove the head, on which the mantle was held. It was a tricky operation to manage this without damaging the mantle itself, for the mantle was very fragile. I was sure that someone, somewhere, had invented these contraptions with the malevolent intention of blighting my young life. But my mother left the work to me for she said that she was not mechanically minded, and my father was away at work. She was wary of asking him to help anyway, for on a couple of occasions when a lamp had proved slow to respond to his attentions, he had lost patience and pitched the awkward lamp out over a hedge and into a sheugh.

Quite early in my life settings of eggs became a thing of the past. No longer were clocking hens to be seen about the house in the spring with big flocks of chickens all around them. I always thought they were lovely, and I was sorry to see them go. First of all their place was taken by a brooder. The brooder consisted of a wooden frame covered with fine netting wire, and standing on four legs, so that it was about three feet above the ground. It was about six feet long, two and a half feet wide and just over a foot in depth. The top had three covers, which could be lifted off, and the chickens lived on the netted floor of the structure. There were dividers so that when the chickens were very young they could be confined to a small section, and then this area could be extended as they grew. When mother announced that we could not live without a brooder, my father decided that unlike the neighbours, he would make one, and he did. This proved to be a double boon for my mother, for if things were going well she claimed that it was due to her good care, but if things were not so good, it was due to the fact that her brooder was home made, and not up to the job.

Since there was now no mother hen, heat had to be provided, or the little chicks would die. Oil lamps or heaters of various types could be bought to provide this heat but like the tilley lamps, which came after them, they proved to be temperamental in the extreme. First of all it was difficult to ensure that they were giving out the right amount of heat, and then one had to check them every hour or so to ensure that things had not changed in the meantime. It involved getting up three or four times a night, and my father swore that they were more bother than a baby, and in fact he said you'd be better with a set of triplets. Then the heaters could go on fire, and burn the whole place, they could go out and the chickens would die of cold, or they could start to give out fumes, which would poison all about the place.

The chickens now came in hundreds, in boxes with holes in the sides, from a strange place called a hatchery. And the one thing that I could never understand was that they were all pullets, or at least they were supposed to be. There might be two or three roosters in a hundred but that was all, and it was a mistake. They had been sexed. I spent many hours examining young hens but I never could find out how someone could tell the difference between a male and a female chick. Calves were no problem, dogs and even cats were obvious too, but the chicks had me totally puzzled, and I came to the conclusion that it must be magic. The boxes arrived on a Tuesday morning in Benburb, on the bus. My mother knew that the bus came at half past ten but she would have us waiting from ten o'clock, so that she could get the chicks home and into the heat, as soon as possible. If Da could get the time off he brought them home for her on the carrier of the bicycle, but usually she wheeled them home on my old pram, and it was lovely to hear them all chirping away in their boxes.

In the brooder they needed food and water as well as heat. This was given in round metal dishes with towers in the centre. The meal was put into the towers, and it filtered out into the feeding area through holes, so that as the chickens stood around the dish and ate, the meal was replaced all the time. But this also created a problem. There was nothing a hungry rat loved more than a nice young chick, garnished with some lovely meal and washed down with a nice drink of water. Many a night my mother would wake up and declare that there were rats at the chickens, and my father would have to go out and make sure that everything was all right. He swore that hens were the curse of a man's life, and that the people in London and Glasgow did not know how lucky they were, for they could go down into the air raid shelters and at least get a night's sleep.

Then there was the cleaning of the eggs. Each one had to be cleaned individually and my mother was never satisfied until they were perfect. Once when she was sick, my father and I washed the eggs all at once in a big bucket of soapy water, and they ended up getting better grades than usual. But mother discovered what we had done and she scolded for weeks, for she said it was not fair to the 'crayturs' who had to eat them. For a few years, during and after the war, eggs were very profitable and she made good money. But then things changed and having put up with hard work and no money, my father took action one evening. "Look Sarah," he said, "I have been thinking this long time. I have been keeping an eye on what we're paying for meal and stuff for those bloody hens. I have come to the conclusion that I'm working to keep them, and if things go on the way they are, they'll put us out of the place. I know you made good money for years and years, but there's no damned way I'm going to work to keep hens. I'm sorry but they'll have to go. You can keep a few about the house for our own use, but you'll have to get rid of all the deep litter ones."

Never in my life did I feel such a surge of admiration and love for my father. I could have thrown my arms about him and kissed him. I thought he must be the wisest man in the world. My mother put up a bit of an argument, but my father knew he was right, and there was no changing his mind. She knew he was right too, but I think the fact that she kept hens made her feel important, and it was hard for her to admit that they were useless. So to my utter delight it was decided that the great majority of them had to go, and there was joy in my heart when they disappeared up the lane in the fowlman's lorry. She did keep a few dozen, and sold eggs when she had them, and in fact the last time I saw her alive, many years later, she was rubbing an egg with a piece of sandpaper to clean it, for washing had been banned, and this new method brought in.

The turkeys were a different problem. They were not too bad when they were little birds in the late summer, but when they got big it was my job to bring them in at night and see that they were safely locked up in the shed. I especially remember one particular evening, when I was about ten. We had a flock of about fifty turkeys and there were a number of very big roosters on them, and my mother was delighted for there was a good price for turkeys that year. Nowadays people buy hen turkeys at Christmas, but at that time everyone wanted roosters, because they were much bigger and much more profitable. It came to November and they were a really fine flock of birds, led by one really big rooster.

One evening of drizzling rain, I went to fetch them and found them at the furthest point of the land. I gently brought them up to the house, and had them nicely coaxed to a spot on the street about twenty yards from their shed. At that point the leading rooster took a crooked fit, and went flying round a clump of bushes and back down the field, leading the whole flock back to where I had first found them. That was frustrating. I followed them, and with a lot more bother this time, I got them back to the same place near their shed. Again the rooster took off with the whole flock after him, and by now my temper was really wearing thin. I went into the house and got the sweeping brush, and set out to fetch them.

This time they were really disturbed, and I had a lot of trouble getting them anywhere near the house. Again we came to the clump of bushes, and even though I did my level best to stop him, the rooster took off again. He was flying across the garden in which my father had potatoes, when I fired the brush at him. I didn't really mean to hit him, but the brush caught him full on the back of the neck, and he fell like a stone. The big turkey was dead. I hid him in the potato drills, and went to fetch the others. I managed to get them into the house this time, and then went to approach my mother, "Ma, I've counted the turkeys four or five times and there's one missing. I can't see it anywhere." I was trying to emphasise my diligence and made sure not to mention what had happened.

My mother came out to the shed and she counted them. She counted them a second time with great care, and then she said, "It's the big rooster. He's the best bird in the flock. He must be twenty pounds weight, and what'll he be like by Christmas? We'll have to get him." We searched everywhere. Just as my father arrived from his work, I managed to discover him in the potato drill, and shouted that he was there, dead.

My mother came over and looked at him. She bent down and felt him. She examined him. "Oh God," she said, " I don't know what can have happened to him, and him the finest bird about the place. I hope it's not some disease that going to go through the whole flock and wipe them out." My father came walking slowly and quietly across the garden. He lifted the big bird and holding his legs in one hand, ran the other hand over him. "This bird is still warm," he said. "His neck is broken. He has no disease. I'll hang him up and bleed him and we'll eat him ourselves." My mother looked at him in stunned silence, and so did I. Then my father turned to me, still holding the bird. "I didn't know you were as good a shot with a sweeping brush, Arthur," he said. "You hit him dead in the back of the neck, and you broke it, clean as a whistle."

I was flabbergasted and scared stiff. I could not work out how my father was able to tell me exactly what had happened, for he had been at least a mile away at the time. My mother was annoyed and angry. "Jesus, Mary and Joseph," she cried, "What's going to become of us all? Why did you kill the turkey? Don't you know we need the money coming up to Christmas and he's the best of the flock? Are you going to put us out of the place or what?"

I decided that in this particular instance, the truth might be good policy, just for once. I explained exactly what had happened, and how it had been a kind of accident. My mother seemed about to explode, but my father put his arm round her shoulder and smiled. " I know how awkward turkeys can be Sarah," he said softly. "The cub lost his head and fired the brush in annoyance. It's not the end of the world. The bird has got no harm, and we'll have a big dinner like the rich people this year, even if it's a bit early. Come on into the house now and we'll all have a drop of tea." At that point he put his hand into his pocket and took out a big white fiver, which he gave to her. "I did a bit of extra work this week at the scutching," he said, "and this should make up for the loss of the turkey."

I thought my father was a very wise and understanding man. But ever since that day I've never had a great affection for turkeys.

CHAPTER 7
THE WHITE OWL'S NEST

"Hi boy, and where do you think you might be going to at this time of the night? It seems to me that about all you need is a bit of a stick, and a bundle of clothes tied to the end of it, so that you can carry it over your shoulder."

My father was annoyed and cross, for he had discovered me sneaking away from the house, just after midnight, on a beautiful night of full moon in summer. I had pushed up the bottom half of the window of my bedroom, propped it open with a strong piece of stick, and jumped out into the yard at the back of the house. However, Trimmer the dog had been lying asleep, just under my window, and he let out a fearful howl when I landed on top of him. He must have thought that I had been overwhelmed by a sudden desire to assassinate him for he ran round the yard with his head in the air, howling at the moon. The startled hens, had been roosting quietly, and were disturbed and frightened, and the entire yard was a cacophony of noise.

"What under God is the matter here at all, Mick?" My mother appeared beside my father at the door, and she asked him the question with a mixture of puzzlement and fear in her voice. He stood on the doorstep in his bare feet and replied without ever taking his eyes off me. "That's exactly what I'm trying to find out, Sarah. This young fellow of ours seems to have some objection to using the door, and he has got out of the window of his room, and it looks as if he's heading for Belfast or somewhere, by the way he's dressed and all. Maybe he wants to see what the bombs are like, that we heard dropping a few nights ago. I asked him five minutes ago where the devil he thinks he's going, but the devil must have got a hoult of his tongue, for it seems it's going to be morning before I get an answer."

Now there was a very definite edge to his voice, and the last part of his answer to my mother's question, was very clearly also a warning to me to come up with an answer, and quickly. By this time the dog had recovered from his shock and came up to me, his tail still between his legs, and licked my hand to show that he did not hold any spite at me for having jumped on him. Or perhaps he was trying to ensure that I did not make another attempt on his life. I looked at my parents in the moonlight, and I tried desperately to think of some reasonable explanation that would explain why I was wandering about the street in the middle of the night, when I had been put safely to bed more than two hours before.

"I thought I heard the old fox back at the hens, and I wanted to see if I could catch him, or maybe stop him from taking a couple more of them." My father padded over to where I was standing, treading the gravel carefully in his bare feet. He took me by the ear and led me back to the door, where my mother was waiting. He exerted a steady pressure on the lobe, but he was very strong, and I feared for a moment that I was about to part with a vital part of my anatomy.

"Maybe, my fine lad, you would like to explain to your mother and me, how it is that you are fully dressed and all prepared for the road, if you were in such a rush to save the hens. You have to understand that your mother and me are not too smart, and we never spent too much time at school, and it's hard for us to work out puzzles like this one."

I had not thought of this at all even though it was so obvious, and I knew from the sarcastic tone of my father's comments, that I was now in real trouble. Clearly if there had been a threat to the hens I would have rushed out in my night clothes, and the door would have been the quickest and easiest way to reach the hen's shed. As well as that I would have called my father, for I would not have faced the fox alone. My mother took a hold of my other ear, and I thought for a moment that they intended taking me to the gallows, which I had been reading about, in the neighbouring townland of Lisnacroy. Visions of bodies swinging from the gibbet in the moonlight flashed across my mind, and I feared that I was in great danger of joining them.

"Now, my fine wee son, will you tell us the truth about what you were up to. Your father has a lot more to do than run about after you in the middle of the night. He has a long, hard day's work tomorrow, and he needs a good night's sleep, even if you think you don't." My mother's voice was calm, quiet but firm, and there was a look in her eyes in the moonlight that suggested my explanation had better be good.

For some weeks before this incident there had been a group of ceiliers in my granny's house almost every night. This was unusual for the time of year, but my granny, my father's mother, had been very ill in her home in Drumay, which is about two miles away from our house. Two or three times a week my father would go down to sit with her, and most times he would take my mother and me along too. I really enjoyed those nightly walks with my parents, especially on bright, cloudless nights, when the whole countryside was resplendent in the moonlight.

Tom Jordan, Tommy's father, had been present on one of these occasions, and he had been very explicit about his wonderful experiences when meeting the little people around Sessiagh fort. He described in detail the wonderful music, the dancing, and the sumptuous banquets, which the fairies produced for him in a great hall that they had in the middle of the fort. Apparently oblivious of me, he explained that only the eldest son of an old Irish family would be made welcome at such a gathering. That was why he could be their guest as often as he wanted, on the night of a full moon in summer.

I had decided then and there that on the next night of a full moon, I would visit this mystical place and people, for I too was the eldest son of an old Irish family. And so it was that my father had caught me trying to escape from the house in secret. I did not want to reveal my purpose to anyone. "I could not sleep and I thought

I would take a walk in the moonlight. I was thinking that maybe the wee badgers would be playing about at the bottom of the low field. I wanted to see what they were like. I jumped on the dog when I got out of the window, and frightened him, and he scared all the hens. I'm sorry for starting all the noise."

Both of them let go of my ears at the same time and that was a big relief. My father looked down at me and I could see that there was a lot of suspicion in his eyes. But he must have decided that there was nothing much more that he could do, so he told me to get to bed as quickly as I could, and let people get a night's rest. I went off to my room and slipped into bed, fully dressed, except for my shoes, and pretended to go to sleep. I lay looking at the ceiling, conjuring up all sorts of landscapes from the changing patterns of light and shadow on the boards. I was trying desperately not to fall asleep.

As I lay there, hardly daring to breathe, I could hear my mother's feet padding up the corridor to my room. The door opened gently and without opening my eyes, I was aware that my mother was standing inside the door looking at me. I thought of giving a long loud snore to assure her that I was in deep slumber, but I decided it was better to just lie there quietly and breathe normally.

Eventually she turned and closed the door gently, and I could hear her slipping back to her own room and then I heard the click of the latch as she closed the door. Again I lay looking at the ceiling and debating with myself as to whether I should go or put it off until another time. Finally I decided that since I was dressed anyway, and there was not likely to be a better opportunity, I would go ahead. Again I slipped out of bed and put on my shoes. Quietly I got up and tip toed over to the window. Very carefully I lifted the bottom half, which my father had put back in place, and slid a second prop under it. I had one leg out of the window when Jordan's donkey, which was in the field right beside our house, decided to give a long, loud bray that would have wakened the dead.

In my haste to get back to the bed, I knocked the stick from under the window frame, and it crashed down with a bang, that sounded like a bomb in the small room. In the yard the hens all started to cackle once again, the dog began to bark too, and a thousand crows, which had been roosting in the beech and ash trees, rose into the air and cawed like mad while circling the house. "Jesus, Mary and Joseph, Mick, what has happened now?" My mother sounded a little frightened and I presumed a little angry too.

" I don't know, but whatever our boy is at, he must have been trying to get out of the window again. It looks to me as if we're going to have to tie him in the bed. I'd love to know where he has a notion of going to, but he's going to make damned sure that he's not going to tell us." I could hear the two of them hurrying out into the yard. I jumped into the bed, pulled the clothes up round my neck and hoped it would look as though I had not moved for a long time, and that I was sound asleep and had not heard a thing.

My parents opened the front door and went out onto the street again. I could hear them making their way round the back and into the yard, until they were outside the window of my room. "There doesn't seem to be anything wrong, Mick. I wasn't sleeping and I think that old Neddy took a notion to bray," said my mother.

"He'll be braying somewhere else from now on," replied my father angrily. "I'll get Tom to put him in the far hill and he can bray all night there till his heart's content. But there was a big crash from our boy's room and it sounded that he had the window up again and he let it drop. He's up to something whatever the hell it is. This is some time of the night for us to be traipsing about the street, like two eejets escaped from the asylum."

I could hear them coming in through the front door, and I hoped that they would go off to bed without checking on me. But then I heard the feet padding towards my door and I did my best to show that I was sound asleep. They opened the door of my room and stood in the middle of the floor, looking down at me. After a few moments the door was pulled shut, and I breathed a huge sigh of relief. I was just about to pull back the bedclothes when the door slammed open and my father stood in the opening. I could see him through my closed eyelids for the bright moonlight shining through the window, picked him out like a spotlight on a stage. I wondered why he had come back and I did my best to breathe evenly as though in a sound sleep.

He stepped forward at last and with his right hand caught the bedclothes and whipped them clean off the bed, leaving me exposed and lying with all my outdoor clothes on. I still pretended to be asleep but my brain was working overtime, trying to think of some good reason as to why I was fully clothed, and wearing my shoes in bed.

"And since when did you start going to bed with all your clothes on my young man? Is this some new fashion that I have not heard any news of?" My father asked these questions as if I had been sitting up in bed talking to him. It was clear to me that he knew that I had not been asleep since he had first seen me in the yard. I looked up at him and pretended that I was finding it hard to see him or to get the sleep out of my eyes.

"What's the matter? Who is it? Is the house on fire or what?" I shook my head, rubbed my eyes and tried to look at my father as though he were still coming into focus. "Oh, it's you Da, What time is it? I must have been dreaming. Is it time to get up for school?"

My father sat down on the bed and when he looked into my eyes the annoyance that was glowing in his eyes assured me that I had not fooled him. He slowly raised his right hand and I jumped over to the wall for I was sure that he was going to hit me, a thing that he had seldom done in his life. But he only rubbed his ear and his hair and then lowered the arm again. All this time he was staring into my eyes.

"Now, maybe we should start over again," he said very softly but firmly. "You have been up to something and you might as well tell me why you want to go out gallivanting in the middle of the night. If you don't need any sleep your mother and me do. So now let's have the truth and then we'll forget all about it."

I don't know why it happened but I had a brainwave. I looked straight into my father's eyes and I was sure there was a look of total innocence in my own eyes, as they flashed at him in the bright rays of the moon. "Och, Da, I was going out right enough and I'm sorry for telling you a bundle of lies. I wanted to find out where the big white owl has her nest. I think she might have young ones in that big ivy tree that is near the back of the barn. Every night she hoots and hunts round the yard, and I think she must be hunting mice or rats to feed the wee ones. I would love to get a look into the nest to see what it is like, and to see what the young ones are like."

My father looked down at his feet, and then he looked sideways at me and then he started to laugh. I knew that I had won the battle, and that his anger was gone. "Now, now, is that all it is? Why didn't you tell me and I would have given you a hand? I'm, tired tonight and I have a big day's work tomorrow but some of these nights we'll go out and see what we can see. Now up you get and get ready for bed." He stayed sitting on the edge of the bed and there was nothing I could do but carry out his wishes. Only when I was tucked up in bed again and drifting off to sleep did he move. I decided that my visit to the little people would have to wait till another time.

I was all but asleep when I was aware of my father outside my window. In his hand he had a hammer and he hammered in a nail about five inches below the edge of the top sash. The window would now open downwards a little to let in air. Seconds later the door of my room opened and he padded over to the inside of my window. About five inches above the edge of the bottom sash he hammered in another nail. It was now impossible to open the window enough to get out through it. He stood back and admired his handiwork. Then, apparently talking to himself, he said, "You can never trust those owls especially those big white ones. That'll keep them from coming in and out as they like. I have a feeling that for some time to come we're going to get a decent night's sleep every night. Our boy will need the help of the fairies out of the fort, if he wants to go wandering again."

I fell asleep wondering about my father's last words. But to this day I am not sure if he knew that I was going to see the fairies, or if it was just a chance remark.

My mother, Sarah Daly, (nee Bloomer) as a young woman. c. 1930 in Glasgow. She first came to Sessiagh in 1933 and was married in September of the following year.

CHAPTER 8
BREAKING INTO BARNEY'S

In the years during, and after the Second World War, a number of vanmen called at the houses in our townland, almost every day. Most days there was at least one breadman and then there were a few carts, which carried a large range of groceries. Each of the housewives had her own preference amongst these, and while a woman might deal with all, or most of them, she reserved the bulk of her purchases for her own particular favourite. In my earliest memories some of the carts were horse drawn but one or two were motorised. The men with the horse drawn carts must have had a very hard life, for they sat on top of the cart at the front, with absolutely no protection from the weather. The last such vehicle to survive in our area was an 'Inglis' breadcart, driven by a hardy little man called Bobby Pinkerton, and he still had a horse well into the fifties. He was certainly one of my mother's favourites but he had sharp competition from a general grocer called John Nesbitt, and a breadman called Joshua Greer.

The Glow of the Oil Lamp

I cannot remember a time when John Nesbitt's red cart did not call at our house on a Thursday, and he was still calling when I was well into my teens. Like John, Joshua had a motorised cart, and while he was officially a breadman he carried all sorts of goods to order. But he had the life and soul scared out of my mother, for he was always warning her that if the police caught him he might well end up in jail, and she was afraid that she might have to go with him. It was clearly a secret business, which he carried on, unknown to the firm, and my mother must have been one of his best customers. All during the war it was almost impossible to get tea or sugar. Butter would have been a problem for town dwellers, but we made our own, so we could actually sell some. But my mother bought sugar in stones and sometimes in half hundredweights from Joshua, under a vow of total secrecy and at truly exorbitant prices. She was always warning me never to mention to anyone that we were getting things on the black market no matter where I was. She also bought tea in pounds so that almost every week there was some sort of underhand dealing going on, and I think she took a great delight in it, even if it cost her a fortune.

Wednesday was the day on which the eggman came. The eggs had to be packed on cardboard trays, which held two and a half dozen each, and then these trays were fitted into a wooden case. The case was divided into two halves with six trays fitting into each half, so that a full case held thirty dozen eggs. My mother usually had two or three cases to sell each week. In the autumn, for about a month, the eggman also collected blackberries.

The blackberries were ripe in September and for a few weeks the women and children of every household, spent their spare time collecting blackberries from the hedgerows around the townland, and sometimes further afield. They were stored in buckets, tins and baths and there was always great excitement on a Wednesday to see the fruit weighed and loaded on the lorry. It was an activity, which provided some welcome extra cash, and was a way in which the children could augment the family income.

Every year from we were six or so, Tommy Jordan and I collected blackberries, often aided by our mothers. Sometimes the women would build up a substantial collection of their own, and sometimes they would simply augment ours. There was a friendly rivalry between us to see who could have the biggest lot by the time the eggman came each week, and, likewise there was also an undeclared war between our mothers. As the years passed, Tommy and I learned where the best clumps of briars were to be found and apart from a few hedgerows around our own houses, we shared all the favourite spots. These were usually to be found in and around the fort, and in a deep valley which lies to the east of it and which stretches all the way to the Moy road. It was tedious and prickly work but we enjoyed it, we enjoyed each other's company, and most of all we enjoyed getting a few shillings each week.

It was coming towards the end of the blackberry season one year, and all the choice spots had been stripped bare. One evening we set off together after school and decided to investigate the hedges, which lay to each side of the lane beyond the lough. It was a glorious sunny afternoon, and just after we had passed the lough we came to Joe Allen's hills. Here a group of neighbours were building Allen's corn into pecks, to be ready for the coming of the thresher, in a few weeks time. Some men were drawing in shigs of corn with horses and floats, and some were pitching the sheaves up to the peck where my father was building. As we passed, the peck was already pretty high and one man was perched on a ladder, taking the fork with a sheaf from a man on the ground and passing it upward to my father to be placed and tramped into its proper position.

There was a constant banter amongst the men, and when they saw us, work stopped for a few minutes, so that they could enquire as to how we had got on at school, whether we had got any slaps, and if there had been any good fights. They also talked amongst themselves about wee fellows they knew, who had collected so many blackberries that the eggman's lorry was not able to carry them, and he had to come back a second time for the rest of the load. But they emphasised that these were very good blackberry pickers, and nobody in our part of the country could hope to match them. We continued our search with a bitter taste in our mouths.

We reached the end of the lane little the richer for our search. Here, at the junction, where the Sessiagh lane meets another road, Barney, Tommy's uncle, had bought a farm some time previously, and although not married at the time, was living in the little cottage. It

The Glow of the Oil Lamp

was obvious that Barney was not at home, and having searched an old lane near the cottage, we were about to head for home. Tommy and I came out of the orchard in front of Barney's cottage, and Tommy eyed the building with interest. "What would you think," he asked, looking me right in the eye, "if we went into Barney's and made a drop of tea. Surely Barney would not mind at all if we made ourselves a drop of tea?"

We left down our blackberry tins on the front door step and tried the door. It was firmly locked and no amount of pushing and shoving could budge it. We searched all round the doorstep but there was no sign of the key anywhere. We tried the windows, which were the old style wooden ones, which slid up and down on their sashes. The one on the lower side of the door would not move, but the one on the upper side pushed up easily. But when I tried to get through it, it slid down again and trapped my back so that I could not move. Tommy managed to force it up so that I could escape but he could not hold it up long enough for me to get through. "That bloody window is as awkward as bloody Barney himself," said Tommy, "I doubt that we're going to have to do without any tea."

But Tommy had put the notion of making tea into my head, and I went off to the orchard, which was in front of the house and across the lane. Barney must have been pruning apple trees the previous spring, for there were lots of cut logs lying about all over the garden. I picked one out, about four inches in diameter, and about fourteen or fifteen inches long. I brought it back to the window and when Tommy pushed upward,

I placed the stick under the frame. It fitted perfectly. We managed to climb through the window and into the house without any trouble at all. We made our way down to the kitchen, but Barney's range was cold and black, and it was obvious that no fire had been lit in it that day. "If we had a few bits of paper and some sticks we'd soon have a blazing fire," said Tommy, "You clean out the grate and I'll see what I can find about the house."

By the time I had the grate neatly cleaned out Tommy was back with some newspaper and a handful of sticks. We rolled the paper into bundles and put these at the bottom of the grate as we had seen our parents do at home and then we placed the sticks in criss-cross fashion on top of them. All we needed now was a box of matches. We searched the kitchen from top to bottom but there was not a sign of a match anywhere. We looked at each other wondering what to do. "I tell you," said Tommy, "Barney smokes the pipe. He's bound to have a load of matches somewhere. We'll go down to the bedroom for there's bound to be boxes of matches in his pockets."

We went down to the bedroom, which happened to be the room through which we had entered. We looked all round the room and searched the drawers and cupboards, but not a match could we find. Tommy opened the wardrobe where Barney had his coat and a couple of suits, neatly hung up. We took these out, one by one, laid them on the bed and went through the pockets but again we did not find any matches. We stood in the room looking at each other in amazement.

"Well, I don't understand it at all," said Tommy, shaking his head, "How the hell could a man who never lets the pipe out, not have a match in the house. I doubt we're going to get no tea today."

We made our way out through the window, gathered up our blackberry tins and started out for home, very downhearted. By the time we reached Allen's hills the peck of corn was finished, thatched and roped, and the men had gone, for it was now quite late in the evening. Not only had we got no tea, but we had very few blackberries to show for our evening's work.

That evening the storm broke. My mother had lit the oil lamp, I was doing my homework, and my father was reading the paper, when in rushed Tom Jordan, Tommy's father. "Damn it all, did you hear the news Mick?" he asked, and without waiting for an answer he went on, "some crowd of damned villains broke into Barney's house the day. They wrecked the place, and went through every article in the house and even pulled out all his clothes. But whatever sort of a crowd of boyos they were, there was a wad of notes in the pocket of his suit and they never took a thing. Now what do you think of that?"

My father left the paper down on his knee and looked up at Tom. "Well, that's a tarra, Tom," he said. "What the hell would take them into anybody's house if they didn't want the money? Maybe they didn't see it."

"Oh they could not have missed it," replied Tom. "Sure they pulled the linings of the pockets inside out, and left them like that and left the money on top of them. What the hell's blazes they were after, is more that I can tell."

"What are you going to do about it?" asked my father. "Are you going to get the police?"

"I don't see any sense in getting the police when there's nothing missing. This is a real hangman's job Mick. I'm going to take the shotgun and sit round at Barney's till they come back. They left a big lump of a stick holding up the window where they got in. I've a good notion that they were disturbed and they'll be back. If they come back I'll give them a warm welcome. They'll not go away, the way they came. Mick, this is a real hangman's job, I tell you."

Tom turned to leave and my father went out with him. In all this time I had not moved, I had hardly dared breathe, and I pretended to be totally absorbed in my homework. But in fact, nobody paid the slightest attention to me. I was trying to work out in my own mind what Tom meant by 'a hangman's job.' I couldn't decide whether it meant that hangmen were always doing despicable acts, or if, when caught, Tommy and I should get strung up. At any rate I was frightened and I wished that I could have a conference with my friend to decide what we should do. It was quite a few minutes before my father came back into the house. "Tom's in a quare state," he said to my mother. "He's away to get the gun to go round and sit all night in Barney's. And he says he's going to stay till the robbers return."

My parents had a long discussion about the whole affair, but by bedtime they had not come to any solutions or conclusions. I was glad to get to bed myself, so that nobody would ask me any questions, but that night I tumbled and tossed and got hardly any sleep at all. When I did doze off I had nightmares in which I imagined a big man with a noose in his hand chasing me over hill and dale, so that I was continually waking up in a cold sweat. I was glad when my mother called me for my breakfast.

When I got up my father was already away to work, and my mother did not mention the previous day's exploits to me at all. I suppose she thought I was too young and innocent to comprehend such matters. Tommy joined me at his house and we set off for school. As soon as we were out of earshot of the house, he turned to me, "Did you hear the hullabaloo that was on last night?" he asked with bated breath. "Da went away round to Barney's and sat all night with the gun across his knees and it loaded. He swore that he'd blow the brains out of the boys that broke in yesterday. I damned near burst my sides laughing."

"Be God, you'll not be laughing if they catch on that it was us that broke into Barney's," I said, " Your Da's for hanging whoever he catches. And he's stone mad with anger."

Tommy looked at me with contempt in his eyes. "How the hell are they going to find out that it was us?" he asked, as if he thought the whole idea was crazy. "If they didn't catch on yesterday, they'll never find out, and our man can sit round there with the gun on his knees for the next year if he likes. There's no chance that he'll find out from me, and you make sure to keep your mouth shut."

The rest of the week passed quietly. Men who met each other on the road talked over the incident but it was too early in the year for ceilying, so that there were no really big discussions about it. I began to think that no one would ever find out what had really happened, and Tommy was absolutely sure of it.

The following Saturday morning I was doing my work in the byre when my father came in. He examined the place and congratulated me on how well I had looked after things. Then he started a conversation about whether or not we should sell a young heifer that had been born the year before and which I had reared. I was in full flow on this topic when in a calm, quiet voice, he asked me, " And what took the two of you into Barney's Arthur?"

"Och, we only wanted to make a cup of tea Da," I said, not realising fully that the topic of conversation had changed. "But we couldn't find a match to light the fire."

I had the whole sentence out before I realised what I had said. I clapped my hand over my mouth and looked up at my father. He was standing, with one shoulder leaning against the wall, and he was absolutely shaking with laughter. He put out his hand and rustled my hair. "Right enough, son," he said, "That was a real hangman's job."

"How did you know it was us Da? The whole country is talking about it and nobody ever thought of us. But Da, we only wanted to make a cup of tea and Tommy thought Barney would not mind at all."

My father looked at me with a big smile on his face. "You know, son," he said, "I have always thought that when everybody is puzzled and there seems to be no answer to something, there is usually a very simple solution staring you in the face. Then I remembered seeing you boys in the lane the day I was building the stack. I came to the conclusion that there aren't two better hangmen in this part of the country."

I looked up into his smiling face and I wondered if I would ever get away with anything with this man who seemed to know everything. But he always seemed to see the funny side of things too.

THE SACRED CYCLE

Beneath the diamond window
In the middle of the jam,
The blue bike lay against the wall
Untouched by any man.
And if I dared go near it
Throughout my childhood days,
Mother'd shout an instant warning
And her face would flare with rage.

At the time few neighbours had a bike
T'was a thing beyond their means,
My father's was a rusted hulk
Huge wheels with great wide rims.
This bike was sleek and slender
With the handles turned down,
And wee fine rims upon the wheels
That no man had seen go round.

My father took it out one day
And he stood it on its head,
He was deaf or just unheeding
To the words my mother said.
He tested it for punctures
And with air the tyre infused,

The Glow of the Oil Lamp

He announced despite the idle years
It was a machine that could be used.

Next day he went to Monaghan
To buy a cure for constant pain,
A neighbour suffered bitterly
And he lived just down our lane.
As to why he took the racing bike
To me he'd never tell,
But he said t'was worth my mother's wrath
To make a neighbour fit and well.

Mother's brother came to claim the bike
He was a man I'd never seen,
Away in Scotland or America
Or in other lands he'd been.
Yet when I met this paragon
Strange thoughts I had to think,
For he sold the sacred cycle
To buy another drop of drink.

CHAPTER 9
TROUBLE IN TAXIS

There were very few cars in our part of the country in the last two or three years of the Second World War. There was not one privately owned car in our townland, nor in any of the six or seven townlands around it. The only people whom I knew who owned cars were the two priests and the two teachers in the school. Such a luxury was unimaginable for the ordinary person at that stage, and I don't think anyone could have foreseen, how things would develop within a very short span of time. There were two or three men who ran taxis, but their hire was seen as a very costly method of travel and only to be used in emergency, or on very special occasions. Going to the chapel on Sunday was seen as a special occasion, and seven or eight women agreed among themselves to hire Tommy Murphy's taxi to take them to second Mass every Sunday, in Clonfeacle chapel. The car was very overcrowded but no one minded too much, as long as sharing the fare made it affordable. As far as I can remember it cost each woman one shilling and sixpence for the return trip.

The Glow of the Oil Lamp

On a couple of occasions, on very bad days, my mother took me along with her to share the taxi. I was pushed in between her and the driver, to sit on top of the handbrake lever, and there was always at least one other woman in the front as well. There were, however, one or two women who always complained that they were most uncomfortable and that children, and especially young fellows should be allowed to walk to the chapel. Apart from anything else the breath of fresh air would do them good. My mother turned a deaf ear to their objections and, much to my annoyance, took me along anyway.

The car always arrived in front of the doctor's house in Benburb about ten minutes before the Mass was due to begin, since it was only a journey of over two miles down to the chapel. The ground is pretty level at that spot, and even if the car were left without a handbrake on, it would not have run away. One Sunday we were all loaded as usual, and Tommy Murphy got out to go to one of the houses, to inquire why a particular woman was late, or if she was coming at all.

I may have moved and released the handbrake, or maybe it had never been put on in the first place. But while Tommy was standing at the woman's door, the car began to move ever so gently, and sudden panic gripped one of the complainers in the back. She was screaming at the top of her voice and claiming that the damned rascal in the front was out to take her life. For once in my life I was not to blame, but the idea struck me that it might be a good idea to try on a steep hill, if the woman were on her own in the car.

The Glow of the Oil Lamp

Tommy sauntered back to the car at his ease, opened the door and pulled on the handbrake. "What are you worrying about?" he asked, "Sure the car only moved a couple of yards and was stopped when I came back to it. There was no danger at all."

"That wee rascal in the front is going to be the death of us all," she yelled. "He's like all the boys I see around here; he can't keep his hands to himself nor leave anything alone. It's a tarra that people have to put up with the likes of him when they only want to get to the chapel on a Sunday. Why he has to be pushed in on top of us all is more than I can understand. We'll take a vote and see if we all agree to get rid of him."

A chorus of voices chimed in on top of each other, to claim that there was no need for a vote. Nearly all the women agreed that I had not been to blame at all, and that no harm had been done. The woman sat in a huff and did not speak for the rest of the day. It was not long afterwards that I got my bike, and had no more need of a lift to the chapel.

My Granny also went to the chapel in a taxi, but she went to the chapel in the Moy and sometimes took one or two of my aunts with her. Before she took ill, I used to go and stay with her for a night or two at the weekend, and so I was brought along in the taxi as well. Her taxi belonged to a man called Andy Bookless from the Moy. He was a big, stout man and he owned a sweet and paper shop in the Moy village. It was a veritable Aladdin's cave with things piled on top of each other up to the ceiling. When he was serving, Andy filled the entire space behind the counter and barely had to move

The Glow of the Oil Lamp

to find anything for which a customer asked. I knew Andy and his wife quite well for one or other of them served me when I walked to the Moy for my comics on a Saturday.

One Sunday morning my Granny, and my aunt and myself walked down the lane to the broad road to get the taxi. Andy drew up and said that he was having a wee bit of trouble with his brakes but things would be fine. We collected some more women on the Moss road and in the Glebe. We came to the Rector's brae, which runs steeply down to the Moy road and meets it at right angles. Andy's brakes failed completely and we screamed down the brae, across the road, over a bank and ended up in a meadow, which is about ten feet below the road. It is hard to believe, but no one was hurt, though everyone was shaken. We made our way out of the field and walked home. It was too late to go to Mass and I suppose most of the women thought that they had said enough prayers for one day.

One woman took particular exception to having had a jolt but as far as I can remember, she didn't get much of a hearing, as everyone else in the car was uninjured and did not complain. Some time later I heard one of the men, who came to ceili in our house, saying that as usual the only thing she lost was her knickers. This puzzled me for I could not see how that would greatly inconvenience her, or even how it could have happened to her in the first place. I asked my mother about it but she said I was to mind my own business.

I got a bit of a surprise many years later, when talking to Molly O'Brien, who lived near the Rector's brae. We were talking about things that happened long ago, and I happened to mention the incident with Andy's car. "Indeed I know all about it," she said. "I was going to the chapel in Clonfeacle on the bicycle, and I had just passed the Rector's brae, when this car came like a bullet out of nowhere, and skimmed the back of my bicycle. If I had been two yards further back, I'd have been killed stone dead."

Everyone had a lucky Sunday, including the woman who was said to have lost the knickers.

Those were the years when there were great shortages due to the war. Since we lived about ten miles from the border, nearly everyone did a bit of smuggling of some kind. There were people who made their living by it, and smuggled in a big way. They were often able to bribe a policeman and 'buy the road,' so that they could take herds of cattle across in one night, or smuggle lorry loads of goods of all kinds. Julia Jordan, my mother and a few of their friends from the village, decided to hire a taxi and do a bit of smuggling on their own account. Some women wanted sugar and tea, some meat, some clothes and some wanted to get new curtains. Money was becoming a little more plentiful.

The taxi, which they hired belonged to a man called Paddy Flood from Blackwatertown, and was not only small, but was old and not in great repair. For some reason my mother decided that I should accompany her on the journey, and so I found myself in my usual position in the front, but in an even more uncomfortable state. The following piece of verse tells the story of the trip. It was one of the verses, which got to the finals of the 'Bard of Armagh, festival of humorous verse,' some years ago.

Paddy's Smuggling Band

At the time when bould Hitler was rampant,
A band of our women went forth,
They were planning, in Paddy Flood's taxi,
To smuggle banned goods to the north.
Now Paddy Flood called it his taxi,
It was stretching the meaning by far;
It had seen the best days of it service
In the years of the First World War.
When Paddy pulled up in the village,
The daylight was starting to go.
By the look of the clouds on the skyline,
You'd have said it was going to snow.
Wee Paddy looked up at the women,
And he spoke with a kind of a squeal,
"I'm running real short on the petrol
And some hoor has stole the spare wheel."
But the women piled into the taxi,
As though Paddy'd ne'er uttered a sound,
The weight made the springs go a screeching,
And the tailboard was scraping the ground.
In the back there was big Jennie Curran,
With the daughter perched up on her knee.
There was old Sarah Carr and the sister,
Mrs Tennyson, and the widow Magee.
In the front as well as wee Paddy,
Julia Jordan, my mother, and me.
We started up the road for the border,
Paddy said he was shivering with fright.
As he edged the car out of the Dyan,

The Glow of the Oil Lamp

In the darkness we saw a red light.
"Ach, be Gawd," said wee Paddy, "it's the B-men,
What the hell am I going to say?"
"You can tell them the truth," said big Jeannie,
"That you're taking us out for our tae."
The policeman gawked in at the window,
And he pushed the cap back on his hair.
"By God," said he, "Them's fine big heifers
They'd make a quare price at a fair."
"Would you tell that wee runt I'm no heifer."
Said Mrs Tennyson with a sort of a growl.
"If you'd let me get out of this taxi,
He'd be mate for the hens, by my saul."
The policeman said, "Go on, and good fortune,
And we crawled through the darkness and hail.
It was an hour and a half from we started,
When we landed in sweet Emyvale.
There, the women took into the shopping,
They bought sugar and tea by the stone.
They bought country butter and biscuits,
And big lumps of beef on the bone.
And when they went into a clothes shop
Jeannie Curran stripped down to her pelt.
Wrapped a hanging of curtains around her,
And fastened them tight with a belt.
And the widow Magee bought new bedclothes,
And she fixed them in pleats round her chest,
Then she looked at herself in a mirror,
Saying, "I'm damned but the widow's still the best."
Getting back in the car was a problem
With the women, their wrappings and stuff.
"God help my poor car," said wee Paddy,
"The wee craytur's had more than enough."
In the back there was Jeannie, now bigger

The Glow of the Oil Lamp

With the daughter perched up on her knee,
There was auld Sarah Carr and the sister,
Mrs Tennyson, and the widow Magee.
In the front on the top of wee Paddy,
Julia Jordan, my mother, and me.
As we headed down the road from the border,
There was hardly one uttered a word.
They were saying their beads at each corner,
They'd developed great faith in the Lord.
But when we got near to the village,
The widow called out with a shriek,
"These God damned big sheets have me smothered,
Look, the sweat's running down on my cheek."
Big Jeannie gave a jerk and breathed out then,
Saying , "some of you think you are bad,
But I'll tell you with these bloody curtains,
Even breathing's a bit of a lad."
Then Julia spoke up right beside me,
Saying, "I've never seen such a sad lot,
To hell with your sheets and your curtains,
My tea's wet and I haven't a pot."
When we got to Benburb it was snowing,
Poor wee Paddy pulled up with a sigh,
When the women had emptied the car there,
There was stuff on the ground four feet high.
Along the street then came auld Dickson,
He was head of the police at the time.
He looked at the goods and the women,
Saying, "I think I have scented a crime.
This stuff has all come from the border,
It is seized in the name of the king.
If you want these things back in the morning,
Twenty pounds to the barracks you'll bring."
"Well, if that don't beat all," said my mother,

The Glow of the Oil Lamp

> "You can say what you like so you may.
> But all we have left for our bother,
> Is a drop of poor Julia's wet tae."

I only went on this one trip to the border, but I can't remember how many my mother took part in. After I got my bicycle, Tommy and I used to go the Mullan's Mill every second Saturday. It was a small hamlet just across the border, but it had a grocery shop, where one could buy all the goods that were unavailable in the north. It was about ten or eleven miles from our homes but we didn't mind, in fact we enjoyed the journey on our bikes. There was always the chance that we would be stopped and all our goods confiscated, but in all the times we went, no one ever bothered us.

There was a police constable based in Benburb at that time, whose name was McCaughey. He spent a lot of his time on night duty, on the roads near the border, and in the eyes of the authorities, it was his job to put a stop to the smuggling. He did take an immense amount of goods of all kinds from people whom he stopped, but very little of it was handed in to the barracks. His wife had a motorbike with a sidecar, and in the daytime she travelled round the countryside, selling the stuff that he had collected during the night. The sidecar was always loaded. She called with my mother now and again, and mother would complain that it was a disgrace, the way that the two of them were robbing the people of the country. At the same time she always bought goods from her on the black market, and that did not seem to trouble her conscience. The two of them used to sit chatting in a very friendly way while they shared a cup of tea at our fire. Mother always had an eye for a bargain.

Our trips must have cost Joshua Greer a fortune, because I can remember hearing my mother telling my father that the things we brought from Monaghan, only cost her half as much as she had been paying at the door. The need to hire taxis to smuggle, was a thing of the past.

The doctor's house in Benburb in front of which taxis stopped to collect women for church or to go on smuggling expeditions.

CHAPTER 10
THE GLOW OF THE OIL LAMP

The long days of the year were spent roaming the hills and valleys, and the long nights were spent listening to the five or six men, who always came on their ceili to our house, once autumn was well established. They were neighbours who sat round the fire swapping stories or news, and most of all just enjoying each other's company. The news sometimes centred on the course of the war, but was much more likely to concern the fortunes or misfortunes of those in the locality, especially if there was a comical side to the tale, which never lost anything in the telling.

They gathered in, one by one, over the space of an hour or so, soon after darkness had fallen. Each man had his place in the kitchen, gathered round the big open fire. To me there was something almost magical, in the way the blazing fire cast light and shadow on the faces of the men. The fire seemed to me to give more light than the little double burner paraffin lamp, which hung on a nail on the wall behind them. My father always occupied the armchair in the corner to the right of the fire, and my mother had a little chair of her own, opposite him on the left. She always spent the evening sewing or knitting, listening, but seldom taking part in the conversation. She also spent the time watching the big pot, which was hanging on the crane crook above the fire, full of potatoes to feed the hens, next day.

There was Barney from next door who had been all over the world and who was an authority on things far beyond the knowing of the ordinary men. He had managed to get a wireless set and he had lots of news, which was new and exciting. Sometimes he would invite a few people in to hear the news, or to listen to "Round the Fire" on Athlone. In his discussion he could refer to great men who lived long ago in places like Greece or Rome, and he would quote them to strengthen his arguments. I was especially interested, because my teacher in Benburb school at the time, gave us a lesson on ancient Rome for an hour each week, and I found many of the names or places turning up in Barney's talk. It often puzzled me as to why it was my father who could often quote others in return, in order to scupper or support Barney's argument. It seemed a strange thing for a stupid man to be able to do. Sometimes the argument would turn to religion and my father could quote the bible to suit himself, no matter which side he was on, so that Barney would get agitated and say, "You would think that you had written that damned book yourself, Mick, for you seem to know it by heart."

Barney also had stories of working in butter factories in Australia, and told how he had a big welt across his tummy from leaning over a great vat, to stir the margarine with a big thing like the oar of a boat. I can still feel the skin crawl on my body as he told of going to swim one day, and how a shark came and took away the whole bottom half of the man who was beside him. Barney fought with the beast for the other half, and as he struggled to drag it ashore, the triangular fins of other sharks were like a thousand small boats in the water, for the place was red with blood.

There was Joe who smoked a pipe and who mesmerised me with the way he could cut the tobacco, and hold it in his hand and roll it without spilling a bit. There was a long slow procedure for filling the pipe before lighting it with a big red ember from the fire, which he lifted with our big long black tongs. Joe spoke so softly that everyone had to keep absolutely silent, and hold their hands to their ears in order to make out what he was saying. Joe lived near the lough, and was always seeing a wee small woman with a long black shawl and a big black dog. And it would often happen too that he would be coming home minding his own business when, in the middle of a field, he would see a great big white dog, which would glitter in the moonlight. The dog would go in front of him till they reached the lough, where it would change into an old woman and head for the island in the middle of the lough.

There was a period when Joe was visiting a widow woman who lived some miles away. Often the trend of conversation would turn to the advantages and disadvantages of courting a widow, at which point Joe would be eliminated from the conversation, and treated as though he were not there at all. There would be prolonged howls of laughter, the reason for which I could seldom understand. But it usually ended up with Joe jumping up and running out in a raging temper, shouting over his shoulder that he wasn't going to listen to a crowd of fecking know alls, that were up to their arses in other people's affairs. This result was greatly to the glee of those left around the fire.

Tom was Joe's brother, and he sat upright and leaned back in his chair when he spoke, and usually found a place at the back of the kitchen. He chewed tobacco and smoked a pipe, and from his seat he could land big spittles all round the huge pot, that mother had on the crane crook. It never ceased to amaze me as to how he managed to hit the back of the fire or the side of the hob or whatever spot he chose, but never the pot. Tom told his stories in measured tones, pausing between each sentence, so that his listeners could get the full impact of what he was saying. His stories were often of the little people, and it would appear that they had accepted him as their special friend. He would usually see them around the fort on a bright moonlit night, and he assured us that their music was magical to the ear.

Tom always led the farming talk, which took up a large part of each evening's conversation. It concerned the price of corn, or cattle, or potatoes or the effect the weather was having. It concerned the state of the crops that year and there was always a comparison with years in the past, often a very long time in the past. There was always some reference to the building of stacks, or other yearly tasks, and it was clear that everyone was an expert in every aspect of life on the land.

A second Barney had a severe stutter and to me he was the most interesting of all. He insisted on talking everyone down, though a big part of his speech was a series of eehs and aahs, which preceded every word he spoke. He could actually speak reasonably well provided no one looked at him while he was doing so. But I noticed that Tom, who was one of his brothers, always looked straight into his eyes as soon as he opened his mouth, and then it was a struggle for him to get a word out. The act provided a source of great amusement to all in the house.

Barney had the greatest and scariest selection of ghost stories. And it was because of him most of all, that for years I was heart frightened to go near the lough, even if it was only threatening to get dark. He also had a fantastic memory and could trace families back through many generations to well before the time of the great famine. He knew exactly who had lived in all the ruined houses for miles around and he knew the dates of everyone's birthday, date of marriage, date of death and a thousand other things besides.

Barney had a number of charms, which were guaranteed to cure all sorts of ails or diseases. He had a constant stream of people who came to him because they had sprained an ankle or wrist and when he pulled it, it got better in three days. He had a cure for ringworm, which was an infection that one got from cattle and which was very prevalent in the country at that time. He also had a cure for jaundice, which was apparently so unpleasant to take that my father said, you'd be better keeping the bloody jaundice. The one thing that Barney would not discuss was his potential to cure. If the subject were raised while he was in the company, he would get up without a word and leave the house.

One of my very earliest memories is of a strange incident that happened because Barney took a very bad sty in his eye. I think I was only about three at the time and the whole thing is fairly vague. He came to our house one day and told my mother, "I have a terrible bad eye here, and I want you to get the child here to cure it. He has the power because he is the first of the family to be born since the house went on fire." Barney went out to our front garden, and got a thorn from a gooseberry bush. My mother held me on his knee and she guided my hand as I gently touched the sty three times with the thorn, saying each time, "In the name of the Father, and of the Son, and of the Holy Ghost." Barney swore that the sty was gone in three hours, and indeed as far as I can remember it seemed to be.

During conversations the men seldom looked at each other, nor at my mother or father, but kept their gaze firmly fixed on the fire, where the ever changing shapes of shadow and light in the heart of the glowing coal, seemed to inspire either their imagination or their memory. They also had a particular interest in the pot in which my mother had the potatoes for the hens. She would always open the pot when the potatoes were boiled, and take out a number of the best and biggest. Having replaced the lid she would space these potatoes round its edge, and put more coal or sticks on the fire to give them a good toasting. When everyone was satisfied that they were well toasted, she would set down a saucer of salt and a jug of milk, forks and knives, and some cups. This was the signal for each man to take a potato, and ignoring the cutlery, peel it with the big nail on his thumb, dip it in the salt, and devour it with obvious relish.

The sharing of this simple meal has always remained in my mind as a time of special warmth, when everyone seemed at ease with the world, and would not have exchanged this poor but cosy kitchen for any thing or any place in the world. It was especially cosy when the rain hammered on the tin roof, and particularly when the wind howled around the little house. I know that the men around the fire felt and enjoyed this communal closeness in the soft glow of the oil lamp, and for me it is an aspect of my childhood that I will always cherish.

CHAPTER 11
THE WAKE OF ADOLF HITLER

I knew Jamie Foye from my earliest days. He was a stocky, bustling, restless man, who seemed always to be annoyed about something, or with someone. He called to our house on one or two nights each winter because, years earlier, he had gone to the same school as my father for a short time, and claimed to be his best friend. Da denied this vigorously, but welcomed him all the same, because he said that it was wise to keep in with the bad for the good will never do you any harm. Jamie was not bad really, but he seemed to have a spite at everyone he had ever known, the one exception being my father.

In the long winter nights Jamie joined the five or six ceiliers who gathered around the fire in the shadowy glow of the oil lamp. For the first hour or so it was his practice to remain silent, with his hat pulled down over his face, drinking in the various topics of conversation, which arose in the group. From time to time he would raise his head slightly and glare at whoever was speaking. His eyes glowed with anger from deep within the shadow of the brim of the hat, and to emphasise his

The Glow of the Oil Lamp

annoyance he blew through his moustache as though he were about to explode. It was a sign to those assembled that they were succeeding in getting Jamie going. That of course was the object of the exercise.

Very often the subject of conversation was religion, for Jamie claimed to hate it, and anything to do with it. The priest's sermon of the previous Sunday was a good bet, with some of the men claiming that they had been deeply impressed with it, and that they had never heard anything so novel or uplifting. A couple of others would violently disagree, proclaiming it a lot of rubbish that they had heard a thousand times before. And there were always one or two whose job it was to ask silly questions or make stupid suggestions.

Finally Jamie would push his hat back on his head with his thumb, straighten himself up on the chair, and blow through his moustache to release his pent up fury. "Do none of you bloody idiots ever think for yourselves?" he would roar, stamping his feet on the floor, and waving his arms in annoyance. The knowing winks and satisfied grins that passed among the group were clear to everyone, except Jamie. His eyes were either glued to the ceiling where he seemed to search for solace, or gazing between his feet while he held his hands over his ears.

"This world has more than its fair share of stupid fools and idiots and this part of the country is crammed with them." He gazed at each person in the room in turn, and pointed at each to make sure that they understood that they were numbered amongst these unfortunates. "Everyone knows that I am a genius, an unfortunate genius. The bloody fools that I live among are not fit to recognise a genius when they see one. That does not surprise me for you need a brain to know a genius from a God damned fool. The masters in the school were so bloody stupid and thick that they did not know what they were dealing with. They treated me like any of the other thick heads that were in the school at the time. It's a tarra how thick the people are, and the priests are the worst of the lot, and the ministers that lead those other fools by the nose, are not a bit better."

By this time the two hands would be stretched out in front of him and his voice would be directed between them to the centre of the fire. He would remove his hat with his right hand, wipe it from left to right across his mouth and replace it angrily on his head. Finally the two hands would be placed on his knees and he was clearly ready to explode.

The stage was now set for one of the men to interpose in a simple tone, almost like a child at school. " Yon priest is a quare smart man. Did you hear what he said on Sunday about how people must go to Mass? I wouldn't like to be one of those boys that he talked about that were burning in hell and will never get out. That's only a wee fire that Sarah has burning in the hearth there, and I'll bet you the bould Jamie wouldn't like to sit in the middle of that. God seems to have it in for the boys that don't do what he wants."

Jamie looked at the ceiling and blew through his moustache so loudly that it sounded like a motor car trying to start. Then he would stand up and look around the room at each man in turn, as if he hated the very sight of each one, all the time blowing through the moustache. "You are all a flock of bloody sheep," he would roar. " It's not a bloody bit of wonder that the gospel talks about the sheep and the goats. And it says the goats are worse than the sheep when any bloody wise man knows that bloody sheep are far worse than goats. The priest does not need to be a smart man as long as he can get a crowd of stupid idiots to do what he says."

This was the signal for someone to claim, " The priest has quare powers. I wouldn't like to talk like Jamie here, for it would bring real bad luck on you. I knew a man ridiculed the priest one time and he was dead in a week." That really set Jamie going and the craic lasted for over an hour until he got totally frustrated, and rushed out of the door shouting, "There's no use me trying to talk sense when there's not a brain in the bloody house. If you are all so sure there's a hell, go and stay there and keep out of my bloody way."

Jamie loved to display his detestation of religion in public too, and openly scorned anyone who would say a prayer or go to church. He didn't care which flock they belonged to, they were all sheep, and that is why on a Sunday morning he made sure to have a job to do in his field, which marched the main road. This allowed him to baa over the hedge at all churchgoers and since everyone, either walked or went on a bicycle, it was impossible to escape him. People said that anyone with any sense would ignore the old fool, but it annoyed them all the same. Jamie knew this and it gave him delight to see them wriggling uncomfortably on their bicycles or walking that bit quicker, as he began to baa.

Most mornings it was pretty difficult to get Jamie out of bed, and his wife was often embarrassed when people arrived on the street at eleven o'clock to see if he was coming to finish a job, and Jamie had still not managed to get up. But on a Sunday morning he was up with the larks, so that he could get down to the road to annoy the neighbours. It was almost impossible to get him to do any work in the fields on a weekday, but every Sunday saw him full of enthusiasm.

Jamie was a handyman who would take on hand to do any job that was available. He explained that, while he did not have his time served, he could teach any of the masons, builders, or carpenters who claimed to be tradesmen. Towards the end of the war there was an upsurge in building of all kinds. Skilled men were at a premium and Jamie was called on now and again to do small renovations.

John Crowe lived a couple of miles away and in the last year of the war he decided to build a big shed for the hay, which he called a modern barn. He managed to buy the necessary materials even though that was an almost impossible task due to shortages. He searched everywhere but all the qualified builders were so busy that he was going to have to wait for months, or even a year, to get the job done. Finally he reluctantly asked Jamie, who explained that fortunately he was free at the time.

On a fine Monday around noon Jamie arrived in Crowe's yard, with his tools all attached to his trusty

The Glow of the Oil Lamp

old bicycle. He declared that he had been very busy since early morning, getting all his tools cleaned and sharpened, and that he had developed a bit of an appetite, so that a nice drop of tea and a bite to eat, would be a fine start to the work. Between talking and explaining the complications of such a big job, it was dinnertime before Jamie was ready to get up from the table. There was no use in getting up at that time, since no family would sit down to dinner, and not invite him to join them, so he just stayed on.

Dinnertime was also news time, and the Crowe's had a fine new wireless with a wet battery and a dry battery. On that particular day the news consisted mainly of allied advances and German defeats, all over Europe. As the bulletin developed, Jamie got angrier and angrier so that at last Mrs Crowe had to turn off the wireless, for he was spitting through his moustache and calling the wireless a bloody liar, and was about to demolish it with his fist or his boot. Mrs Crowe knew that Jamie's own wife was fed up getting their wireless fixed after Jamie had attacked it and kicked it into a corner, because the news was not to his pleasing. She was afraid a similar fate was about to befall her nice new one.

The sun was beginning to descend behind the western hills when Jamie got started, for Mrs Crowe had been foolish enough to enquire what the finished building might look like. It took a full two hours for Jamie to do a drawing on the back of a roll of wallpaper, placed on the kitchen table. By the time Jamie was finished she had supplied another three or four mugs of tea. But even then she was none the wiser as to how the building would fit into their yard.

Cement blocks were a new invention at the time and Jamie pointed out that only a very skilled man could use them. The work took more than two months to complete and John Crowe swore that he had counted over a thousand marks of Jamie's thumb in the mortar. Jamie explained that this was a perfectly natural phenomenon in the building trade, since man had hand and thumbs long before he had invented tools. Some of the neighbours claimed that the building was a good bit off the square, to which Jamie retorted that anyone who thought that his building was off the square, must be a long way off the square themselves.

Mrs Crowe claimed that if Jamie did not soon finish the job she would end up like a man, who stood at the gates of Omagh asylum every day. He was of the opinion that all visitors or passers by were patients like himself. He stopped every one of them and asked, "And had you the masons too?" Mrs Crowe said she understood perfectly why he had been there, and she had a good notion to go and join him.

Eventually the building was ready for the roof, and Jamie explained to everyone who would listen, that the putting on of the roof was a job for an expert. There was not one carpenter in the country, who knew how a roof should be cut correctly. A big load of timber had been delivered to Jamie's specifications, and having spent most of a day drawing on the kitchen table, Jamie declared that he was ready to start work. He explained to everyone that it was better to take extra time at the planning stage, since a line on a piece of paper could be rubbed out whereas a plank or joist wrongly cut, was money lost.

Jamie set up a workbench on Crowe's street and proceeded to cut the entire roof there, following the measurements on his drawing. John Crowe enquired if it might not be better to test some of the rafters on the roof, before cutting them all, but Jamie spat through his moustache in bad temper, and explained that only a man who did not know his job would need to do things like that. He was an expert and he did not make mistakes, and Crowe should mind his own bloody business and leave him alone to get on with the job.

It took nearly a week to cut the timber. It was a week that the Crowes were never likely to forget for Jamie informed them that he had got the loan of a mattress, and he was going to sleep under the table since that would save a lot of time. It was difficult for Mrs Crowe to get the breakfast made, with a man sleeping under the table, and relations between herself and John were daily becoming more tetchy. If she tried to slip out to the toilet during the night, she was hailed by a loud grunt or snore from under the table, which sent her back to her room in fear and trepidation. Her lips trembling and her eyes filled with tears, she told the neighbours that she was sure that she would never see the shed finished, and she regretted that it had ever been started.

Eventually the day came when Jamie climbed up on to the scaffolding to fit the roof timbers. The roof tree and the cross timbers gave no trouble, except that Jamie stopped everyone who happened to pass, and

The Glow of the Oil Lamp

explained how difficult a job this was, and how lucky Crowe was that he happened to have the time to do it. He emphasised that no ordinary man should dare tackle it. He came down and put his arm round their shoulders so that when he pointed up, they could not fail to notice how perfectly all the timbers had been fitted.

It was harvest time and John Crowe was drawing a shig of corn to the haggard, when he noticed Jamie starting to fit the rafters. There was clearly something wrong. Jamie was standing on the wall-plate, a rafter in his hand, his hat pushed back on his head. His face was red and he was snorting through his moustache. John could see, even from the place where he had stopped the float, that the rafter was too short. "Have you made a mistake with the timber, Jamie?" asked John anxiously, "I hope you haven't ruined all that timber for it's dear and it's hard to get. What's wrong anyway?"

Jamie looked down angrily, pushing the hat even further back on his head. He blew loudly through his moustache, and as he did so his face got even redder. "Some damned eejet must have changed the figures on the drawings while I was not looking," he squealed. "That's a whole week's hard work down the drain. I'm damned but a man would be better in jail than working about this part of the country, where nobody will leave anything alone."

Looking down at John as though he had altered the figures, Jamie held the rafter in the position where it was supposed to have been, but it clearly lacked a few inches at either end. Then he flung it down on to the street, and standing up to his full height, he addressed the yard in general and John in particular, "Well, no matter what you say, it was hell near it anyway."

John Crowe was normally a very mild, even tempered man but now he was ready to explode. He walked round to the horse's head, took him by the bridle just beside the bit, and looked into his eyes. "I tell you this, Bob," he roared, " You are only a dumb animal, but you have a damned sight more brains than that auld amadan up on the wall. If he is still there when I get rid of this shig of corn, as sure as there's an eye in a goat, I'll take the head off him with the slapping hook."

Jamie must have taken John's threat seriously, for he immediately got down, loaded his bicycle with his tools, and by the time John came back he was disappearing round a corner in the lane, about three hundred yards away. John had to wait until a carpenter was available to finish the job and then it was discovered that Jamie had been timbering the roof for slates, whereas it was to be roofed with corrugated iron. Jamie's explanation for the mix-up was that the Crowe's were so bloody crooked that any brainy man was bound to be driven to distraction and end up exactly as he did. Later on in the year when he called at our house, everyone in the room had so many stupid questions to ask about timbering a roof, that Jamie fled in bad temper and disgust.

Jamie had a son called Bill. Apart from being a little smaller than most people, Bill was quite a bright lad and a good worker. But from Bill's earliest days, Jamie went round the country telling everyone he met, "Our boy's not a hundred per cent you know. He's a bit like his mother's brother, and wants half a brick of a load, you know." The result was that many people tended to treat Bill as rather simple, and when he left school, he could only find the most menial employment at the lowest wages. This state of affairs meant that the young man regarded his father with less than filial adoration.

Soon after Bill left school he began to do weight training, and he put up a punchbag in the garden like the boxer's use. The top spring was fixed to a branch of an apple tree, and the bottom was attached to a big weight buried in the ground. Bill spent hours every week pounding away at his punchbag and practising his weights, and in a few months he was extremely fit and incredibly strong for his size.

The fifteenth of August came around and there was a big day in the village of the Moy. Jamie had spent most of the day in and out of the pubs, and by evening he was not exactly drunk, but he was certainly not exactly sober either. Just as darkness was falling he, and two of his friends were moving from one pub to another, when in front of them, walking down the hill and eating a bag of chips, they saw Bill. In spite of a few snide remarks from his father, for the amusement of his friends, Bill went quietly about his business as though they were not there at all.

Jamie was rather annoyed at being ignored and he skipped up behind Bill, and using his right foot, he pulled one of Bill's legs across the other, so that the lad tripped and nearly fell on his face. The men went into howls of laughter and Jamie was delighted with his handiwork. "Don't try that again," said Bill quietly, turning round and glaring into his father's eyes. "Now I've warned you, don't try it again." His words were greeted with howls of laughter tinged with deep derision.

Bill continued on his way but he had only gone a couple of steps when his father skipped up behind him again and tried to trip him once more. Bill turned round angrily, "Didn't I tell you to stop it. Now I'll not be telling you again." The lad turned to go about his business.

As Jamie skipped up behind him once more, Bill pushed his bag of chips under his left oxter with his right hand. As his father jumped in close to trip him, the lad swung round, and landed a solid right cross on the bottom part of Jamie's rib cage. There was a loud crack that all in the company could hear clearly, and Jamie fell in a heap on the footpath, moaning and groaning. His friends gathered round to see what was wrong, while Bill took his chips in his hand and continued eating them, as though nothing had happened.

"Oh, hell lad, you had no call to do that," said one of the men. "That's your father and you have hurt him badly. It's a damned disgrace, so it is."

Bill stopped with a chip half way to his mouth. He looked at his father squirming on the ground and then at the men. There was a long moment of silence. "You heard me warning him," said Bill. "I warned him two or three times and he would not stop. He thinks he has me for a fool. Well, I'll tell you, if I had hit him the way I meant to hit him, they'd have to sweep him off the road, and carry him home in a bag."

Bill turned on his heel and stomped off. Jamie had to be taken to the hospital where it was discovered that he had three broken ribs. He swore that Bill would never live in the same house as him again, so the lad had to borrow money from an aunt and go to England. Some five years later a neighbour came home on holiday, and informed everyone that Bill was doing well, and was employing twenty two people. Jamie was dumbfounded, but after a couple of minutes a glint of inspiration came into his eyes. "Didn't I tell you all a thousand times," he roared, "that the bloody English are bloody stupid. Well there's the damned clear proof of every word I said." And he blew through his moustache to signal that the argument was settled.

Bread became very scarce during the latter years of the war, and Jamie decided that this was the perfect opportunity to strike a mortal blow at his enemy, Britain. His wife had three hundred hens at the time, and Jamie ordered that, rather than giving them ordinary hen meal or scraps, she should feed them on bread. Thus, at a time when one had to have coupons to get bread, Jamie bought loaves from the breadman in dozens, and at great cost to himself and his wife, he fed them to the hens. It was claimed that the breadman charged him so much for this black market produce, that he was able to build a new house for himself with the profits. When eventually, Jamie had to face the reality that this costly tactic had failed to starve the British into submission, he was forced to sell two fields of his land, in order to clear the debts. At least people surmised that the bread had caused the problem.

People celebrated the end of the war with many demonstrations, marches, and festivals, all over the country. Even though food and many other commodities were scarce, there was a general air of jollification everywhere. One group who organised great celebrations for the victory over Hitler, were the Orangemen, and as is usual with them, they burned an effigy of their enemy in front of nearly every Orange hall in the country.

Our local Orangemen organised a march, a drumming match, and a burning of Hitler just like the others. But the night they chose turned out to be the wettest in living memory. The rain started in the late afternoon and got worse as time wore on. The march was a wash out, the drumming match had to be cancelled, and while a fire was lit under a dummy representing Hitler, the fire could not be sustained, and the whole thing had to be abandoned, leaving the dummy practically intact.

This sequence of events was greatly to the satisfaction of Jamie, who declared that any enemy of the British was his bosom friend. As soon as the activities ceased at the Orange hall, Jamie set out with his bicycle in the pouring rain, rescued the effigy, and with great difficulty managed to carry it home. He said that it was only fair that such a great leader and hero should have a decent wake, and if all the neighbours were too heartless to care, at least he would see that his friend had a memorable send off. It was the least he could do, since our country owed a lot to the German leader. He declared that nearly everyone in the countryside had a lot more to thank him for than he had, but at least he would show them that there was a spark of Irish decency left.

Jamie installed the effigy at the side of the fire, and greatly to the annoyance of his wife, he sat beside it for three days and long into the night. He insisted that everyone speak in hushed tones all the time, and that they remove their hats or caps before entering the house. The news of Hitler's wake spread far and wide throughout the countryside, and there was a crowd of people at Jamie's house every night, the likes of which had not been seen at a wake anywhere before. Jamie was greatly satisfied, and said it showed the respect with which Adolf had been regarded. He was probably unaware that on each of the three nights, there was always a crowd of people holding on to Bill's apple tree, trying to keep their sides from bursting from laughter. Stories of the craic at Hitler's wake were a topic of conversation in the ceili houses for many years afterwards.

There were those who said that Jamie was not motivated solely, by admiration, for a great enemy of the British. They pointed out that when the wake was over, he had half a dozen fine pine planks, which had formed the skeleton of the effigy, at a time when it was practically impossible to get timber anywhere or at any price.

The great ring fort of Sessiagh, looking across Curran Lough from the west. Today academics tell us that this complex of fort and crannóg means that Sessiamagaroll is a royal fort.

CHAPTER 12
DA'S DEVOTIONS

Over the long winters of my childhood in the glow of the oil lamp, there was one story that I heard my father tell over and over again. As he told it there was never a sound in the house, except for the sucking in of breath by his listeners as he reached some very exciting part. I can still see him clearly in my mind, seated in the semi-darkness as he strained in utter concentration to recapture an event, which had taken place a generation before. Seated by the side of the fire and staring into the flames, it seemed as though he were unaware of anyone else in the room. His hands were used to emphasise important points, but it was as though he were talking to the fire. It was an act designed to maintain intent attention and it was incredibly successful. He always told the story as though he were an onlooker, and not the main participant. I can still hear his voice clearly in my mind, as I recall his version of the story:

The rising, swirling clouds of incense were caught sharply, in the rays of the evening sun. Its heavy odour pervaded the little church where the faithful were gathered for evening devotions. The congregation appeared to be grouped very closely around the steeply stepped high altar, because the gallery, which ran round the building, made the place seem to crowd in upon its centre.

Practically every able bodied person in the parish was present, for in those days attendance at devotions was a duty secondary only to attendance at Sunday Mass. Few even of the tough countrymen would dare risk the anger of Fr. Nolan, which could lead to denunciation from the pulpit at Mass, if the explanation were not to his liking. As Joe the sacristan said, after he first brought the priest to the parish in the pony and trap, "He may be a saint but I can tell you that he has a tongue like the very devil himself. Still I will say this for him, he is about as decent a man as ever wore shoes. Do you know that he gave me a whole half crown, when I landed him at the parochial house in the pony and trap?"

"Well," said Big Willie Tully, who had worked for a while in the priest's previous parish, "I'll give you five bob myself, if you undertake to bring him back, and leave him where you got him."

At every opportunity during the devotions the priest's eyes roamed over the rows of kneeling people, searching out anyone who would be disrespectful enough to let his attention wander, or even whisper to a neighbour. Now, as the ceremony neared its end, it was obvious that his gaze was more and more directed to the three rows of seats in front of the high altar, where the children of the parish were located.

Young Mick Dawley in the second row stood for the final hymn, and did his best to meet the priest's gaze

The Glow of the Oil Lamp

with calmness. This was difficult in view of the fact that Charlie Madden, who was directly behind him, had wedged Mick's big toe against the kneeler of the pew. Charlie was one of the few boys who wore boots, and Mick's toe felt as though it was about to be amputated by the hard edge of the leather sole of the big boot. Two or three times he partly turned and showed Charlie his clenched right fist, but the attention of the priest seemed to be instinctively directed to that part of the church, and anyway turning only increased the pain.

The congregation genuflected for the last time and Mick took the opportunity to whisper vindictively over his shoulder, "Madden, I'll burst you."

But the anger in the boy's eyes, and the big fist held menacingly did nothing to release the pressure. In fact Charlie leaned a little harder, and Mick almost cried out in pain.

The altar boys and the priest were disappearing through the vestry door before the first of the young people moved. The painful toe was liberated and Mick moved like a coiled spring and with unbelievable speed. Charlie had been expecting some reaction, but even he was not ready for the tremendous thumping right that caught him just below the rib cage. In spite of himself he let out a loud yell as he bent double under the impact of the punch.

"Stop."

The whole congregation came to a standstill and all turned round to see what had taken place at the front of the church. Fr. Nolan strode purposefully to the sanctuary gate and surveyed the lines of children.

"What is going on here in the house of God?" In the stillness of the church the bated breathing could be heard clearly. Young Mick could feel the sweat begin to ooze between the fingers of his clenched fists. "I ask you before the altar of God, what is going on?" The priest was very calm, standing in his flowing robes, and all eyes were now riveted on the front seats.

"I tripped, Father, and I fell." It was Charlie Madden who answered in barely a whisper, partly because of fear and partly because of the searing pain in his side. "Speak out boy. What did you say?"

"I tripped, Father." This time the young voice could be heard throughout most of the building.

The priest opened the gate of the altar rails and stepped into the middle aisle. He took two steps and stood blocking the exit from the children's seats. Then, turning to the body of the church, he pointed to the door and addressed his people. "Go home in peace, my dear brethren. I will deal with this."

Only the shuffling and the scuffling of boots on stone could be heard as the people gradually made their way towards the exit, many taking furtive looks towards the spot where the priest still held the young people in their places. Looking majestic and terrible in his big colourful robes, he finally spoke in a voice, which carried a sense of power and awe. " And what do you mean by behaving like ruffians in this house of God? Did you not hear what I have been saying on the altar every Sunday for the past six weeks? Do you not know that you are insulting the God, who made you? You should all be ashamed of yourselves. I can tell you that I am certainly ashamed of you.

I have a good mind to make every one of you sit here in these seats, in total silence, for the next three hours."

The children found it hard to stifle a gasp. The half hour of the devotions had seemed long enough on this bright summer evening, so that the idea of another three hours was like an eternity. The lines stood silent, attentive, but a forlorn look began to replace the joy, which had been on their faces only a few short minutes before. At last the priest moved so that he blocked all but the front seat, and pointing to that row he said quietly, "Now march out of the church in silence, and be sure that you genuflect correctly before the altar."

And so it was that within a few minutes they were out in the bright sunlight, which seemed blinding after the dimness of the church. Down at the gate, beside the high graveyard wall, Mick Dawley waited on Charlie Madden. When Charlie went towards the gate, Mick approached him aggressively and blocked his path. "Do you feel like taking me on now? he asked. "Do you think you are as good a man out here, as you were when you were behind me in the chapel?"

Charlie backed off until he was standing with his back against the high wall of the cemetery. He knew that he was outclassed by the slightly smaller, but much stronger boy, and he had no great love for fighting anyway. But he knew too that Mick was hard to stop when a fight of any kind was in prospect, and there was determination in the steel blue eyes, boring into him, that told him he would not get off lightly. He wondered now what on earth had possessed him to torture Mick in the chapel.

There was no movement in the glaring eyes, but suddenly Mick's hand flashed and a straight left caught Charlie full on the chin before he could gather his wits. His head was jolted back with tremendous force. It struck the pebble dash of the wall and big tears came to his eyes. Charlie leaned against the wall and put his two open palms up in front of his face. "Go easy Mick, I'm sorry. I don't know what came over me, the devil must have got me", gasped Charlie. Behind his menacing opponent there was now a ring of eager, excited faces. Charlie had no friends now.

"What the hell's wrong with you now?" growled Mick, "Do you only act the big fella when you're in the chapel and Father Nolan's watching? Put up your fists or I'll give you a loodering anyway."

Charlie had no means of escape. Through his tears he could see the arc of eager faces and the licking of lips in anticipation of a fight. He leaned back against the wall, hoping that some miracle would save him. But there was no escape.

"Well, what are you going to do about it? Are you yellow or what?"

Charlie knew now that he was in a very tight spot. There was no escape from the ring of children, and the insults were cutting very deeply. He wished now with all his heart that he had behaved himself in the chapel, if not for God's sake, then for his own. The big spots of rain brought by the black cloud that had blotted out the evening sun, did nothing to lessen the ardour of his assailant, nor of the spectators. Already the big fist was clenched and poised for action. Terror began to take hold of Charlie and his breath seemed to stick like a lump in his throat.

"And what are you boys up to now?"

At first the question appeared to have come from heaven, but then, looking up, the boys saw Fr. Nolan standing on top of the high graveyard wall, his blackthorn stick held over his right shoulder and his black coat blowing in the breeze. The priest's gaze was directly focussed on Mick Dawley and it had the effect of freezing him in his latest aggressive pose. "I wonder, now," said Fr. Nolan, "if this bout of pugilism would have anything to do with the episode in the chapel."

No one spoke. Some looked down and scuffled their feet in the rough gravel. Suddenly the priest seemed to take flight. For one moment his widespread black flowing garments were suspended in the air above their heads. Then he landed in the centre of the circle, the edges of his long soutane and coat, gliding briskly over the heads and faces of the closest watchers. Hardly had his boots crunched into the gravel, than he grabbed both Mick and Charlie by the backs of their necks, and forced their faces together so that their noses were just touching. There was nothing the boys could do but both felt uneasy and ashamed.

"So there was more to what happened in the chapel than I was told!" Fr. Nolan did not ask but stated a fact, still holding the contestants nose to nose. "Is it not enough shame for you young people, who are

The Glow of the Oil Lamp

supposed to be Christians, to be guilty of such unseemly behaviour in church? Do you have to come out here and disgrace yourselves and your parents in front of the whole countryside? Now shake hands the two of you and if ever I hear of you fighting again I'll break this stick over your backs."

He released the boys' necks but still held the stick horizontally between their noses. Feeling foolish and sorry for themselves they touched hands fleetingly and stepped away from each other. "And now get off home the whole lot of you." The priest turned to the group in general and flung his arm outward so that the stick, now held in his right hand, almost decapitated Charlie Madden where he stood with his back against the wall.

The heavy shower had passed and the sun broke out again. The young people made their way from the chapel gates, separating in various directions. The damp warm road felt comfortable on the soles of their bare feet. Fr. Nolan watched them go, shaking his head and smiling slightly to himself. He then turned into the chapel yard, and began to say his evening office as he sauntered amongst the gravestones.

Mick Dawley and Charlie Madden and a group of younger children climbed the high hill of Stilloga, which led out of the village. From the top of the hill they had a panoramic view of a wide sweep of two counties. Before them on their right lay the gently rolling countryside stretching towards Benburb. To their left the land fell away towards Derryfubble and home. Beyond all this were the haze-blue hills of Armagh, and in the middle distance the twin spires of Armagh's great cathedral rose like twin golden spears into the evening sky. They began to throw stones as road bowls to shorten the journey home.

They came to the gutter, which was a gravelled lane leading from the main road to the hamlet of Derryfubble, and home. Before them and walking hand in hand away from them were Paddy Moore and Winnie Mallon. The couple were known throughout the district to be courting, and this had been the state of affairs now for more than fifteen years. As soon as the couple became aware of company behind them, Paddy let go of Winnie's hand, as though it had suddenly become uncomfortable to the touch, and he skipped nimbly over to the other side of the road. Mick Dawley could not restrain himself from giving a long, loud, echoing cheer, which rang across the countryside and died only slowly among the distant hills of the Glebe.

Paddy and Winnie were now obviously embarrassed. They walked stiffly on opposite sides of the lane and Paddy slowed his pace, so that his girlfriend gradually drew ahead of him. They pretended not to know each other, nor to be aware of each other's presence. It did not help when one of the youngsters shouted, "Go on, ye boy ye Paddy; give her a big kiss, ye boy ye." The others followed up with a loud cheer, which echoed and re-echoed among the surrounding hills. The couple tried walking slowly, then quickly, but their tormentors maintained the same distance and kept up a stream of good-natured taunting. And so it was that they came to Nellie Rafferty's cottage, which was built in a hollow to the left of the road, and had two steps down to the path, which led to the door.

Nellie at this time was an old and sick woman, who had not been seen out of the house for a long time. She was Winnie's aunt, and the talk was that Paddy and Winnie used to spend every Sunday evening courting on the form behind the jam wall in Nellie's house. The old woman was almost totally blind and deaf as well, so the couple had the house practically to themselves.

Winnie opened the little gate that led in from the road, and stepped briskly along the path to the half door. She opened the half door and, standing with it against her bottom, she opened the door and disappeared into the cottage. Paddy appeared to be in two minds. He stopped by the gate and scuffled his feet in the gravel. He played with the latch on the gate for a while. Then, slowly, and apparently unwillingly, he glided down the steps and along the path to the door. As he disappeared through the door there was a great shout from one of the boys, "That's the boy Paddy. She has a big pot of rice boiled for ye and it'll make a man of ye. Give her a hoult, ye boy ye." This was followed by a long, ringing communal cheer.

Quite a few minutes were spent cheering, shouting and cat-whistling. Then, just as Paddy was about to close the door behind him a big sod of turf spattered on the cheek above his head and a shower of fine peat mould covered him from head to toe. Again the boys shouted and cheered for all they were worth while Paddie, never saying a word, disappeared into the house.

The Glow of the Oil Lamp

Out on the road the boys felt lost, now that the objects of interest had disappeared from view. They spent a while clodding turf at the roof of the cottage, but it simply fell quietly onto the thick thatch and made little impact. By this time they had reached the gate and began to dare each other to go through the gate and up to the door, or go right into the hall and peep through the diamond shaped little window that was in the centre of the jam wall. All these activities were undertaken in turn by various members of the group, but they had no visible effect on the couple within the cottage.

Mick Dawley, more than any of his companions, became annoyed by this lack of response. Opening the gate he measured the distance to the doorway, where only the half door was now closed. Then he walked deliberately to the other side of the road, which was wider here in front of the cottage than in other places. The boy tightened his jacket and took a determined, fast run to the top step of the wide-open gateway. Here he took off like a first-class long jumper and flew, feet first, over the half door. His feet landed on the jam wall just below the little window. The other boys, out on the road, stood in stupefied wonder at this athletic performance, and in awe at the boy's daring.

All of the little house seemed to shake under the impact of Mick's weight. But to his horror things did not then turn out as he had expected. The entire jam wall cracked off along the ceiling and in a line, which ran about a foot below the bottom of the little window. The top half of the wall and the boy landed in a cloud of dust and mud on the form where Paddy and Winnie had

The Glow of the Oil Lamp

been sitting beside the fire. All three were amazed and petrified. "Oh, my God," gasped Winnie, "the whole house is down on top of us. Oh God, oh God what has come over us at all, at all?"

Little could be seen in the room with the billowing clouds of dust from the shattered mud wall, mixed with the thick turf smoke from the chimney. All three people tried to get their breath and they coughed and spluttered. Mick gathered himself up as fast as he could and avoided Paddy's attempts to grab hold of him. He successfully made his escape from the ruins of what had been one of the neatest little kitchens in the country. It was a subdued and fearful set of companions who made their way homeward, enjoying little of the countryside as it lay peaceful and beautiful in the late evening sunshine.

There was a grand crowd of neighbours in the Dawley house that night and the craic was good. Again and again the little home echoed to the laughter of the light-hearted country people. But for once Mick did not enjoy any of it. He was all the time waiting for visitors at the door, and it got to the stage where it would almost have been a relief if they had come.

But none did. The laughter and banter and high spirits of the men chatting round the fire only served to increase the heaviness of the boy's mood. That night Mick tumbled and tossed in bed. Sleep would not come. When he did fall into a doze he could see the Rafferty's jam wall crumbling around him again and even the roof of the house seemed to come tumbling down on top of him. Two or three times he wakened his younger brother who slept with him, by jumping up and shouting, "I didn't mean to do it, honest to God I didn't."

It was a relief when at last his mother called him to get up for school. But he had no appetite for his breakfast. He kept a good eye on the lane, which ran down to the main road expecting to see a crowd of Raffertys and Mallons coming to claim damages for the destruction of their home. "What's wrong with you this morning anyway?" asked his mother. "You always have an appetite like a horse, but you have hardly even touched a bite of your breakfast. Are you sick or what?"

The final words brought a thought flashing through the boy's mind. Sickness would mean a day off school and time go wandering over the countryside, or to help his father who was drawing stones and putting them on the county road at this time. Driving the horse was Mick's favourite job, and he would have done anything for a chance to get doing it. But then there was a great chance that someone passing on the road would tell his father what had taken place the previous evening, and he thought it would be healthier for him to be far away when that happened.

"I'm all right Ma. I just don't feel hungry this morning."

"He kept me up half the night, roaring his head off and jumping round the bed. He was shouting like an idiot about somebody going to pull the house down on top of the whole lot of us." Young Luke was sitting directly across the table from Mick when he said this. Mick's foot shot out and he caught his brother a ferocious kick between the legs, just as the boy was getting up from the table. Luke doubled over and uttered a surprised and pain-filled yell. The mother, who had seen what had happened out of the corner of her eye, gave Mick a resounding crack on the ear with the back of her strong, work-worn hand.

"Get out to school, the pair of you, before you drive me mad. I hope that Master O'Connor cuts the tar out of you Mick, for you are getting out of hand altogether. If I ever see you do the likes of that again, I'll get your Da to leather you with his belt and I have a good mind to do it anyway." She turned to lift the big pot of porridge for the pigs, off the crane crook. Her full attention was now given to this task, and Mick was looking sadly at his mother's back. Luke, with his schoolbag in his hand, took the opportunity to skip over and stamp with all his force on his brother's toes before turning, at full speed, and vaulting over the half door and out onto the street. Mick was surprised and the foot was sore but he knew there was no chance of catching Luke, who was the best runner in the school, and had been known to lift a hare on a straight run.

This morning on the way to school Mick did not take the direct road through the Gutter, but went by Scollop Lonen instead. The route was probably a mile longer but it did not necessitate passing Rafferty's. There was the usual fun and games along the way, but Mick was in no mood to enjoy them. As soon as he came up to the school, Charlie Madden and a crowd of other boys gathered around him.

"What happened last night?" asked Charlie.

"What do ye mean? Damn all."

Mick answered as calmly as he could and tried to assume an air of indifference and act as if everything was normal.

"Was there nobody round at the house after you?" Charlie looked as if he were witnessing a miracle.

"Sure weren't ye all in it as well as me," said Mick, "Why should they come to our house when they'd find it far handier to get to yours?"

"We didn't half knock a house down," said Charlie. "I bet ye the Raffertys were round with O'Connor last night and you'll be in for it when we get into the school."

This was an obvious possibility that had never entered Mick's head, and he now felt stumped and stunned, somewhat like a rat in a trap. Coming to school no longer seemed the good idea that it had earlier in the morning, because he would now have the double undertaking of facing the master and his father. It was hard to decide which he dreaded more. In spite of himself he knew that the worry was showing on his face, and he felt he was letting himself down in front of all the boys. Charlie was obviously enjoying the discomfiture of his adversary, and Mick turned on him angrily.

" I know who'll be in for it if you don't close your big mouth," he snapped angrily, and once more his fists and feet took up position for a fight.

At that moment the school bell rang for class and Mick took up his position in the room with his heart in his mouth, and very much aware that he was the object of attention of all the other scholars. But to his amazement the roll call passed off without a word, and one by one the classes passed as well, and by home time neither the Raffertys nor their cottage had been mentioned.

The boys held an inquest into this strange turn of events. There was no doubt that had Master O'Connor known what had happened, he would have taken very strong action indeed, especially since it was clear that he was recovering from an overdose of drink, and was spoiling for trouble. The other days of the week passed just as quietly, and as the time lengthened Mick began to feel more and more secure. He came to the conclusion that Paddy and Winnie were too shy and ashamed, and had decided to keep quiet, and not draw the attention of the parish to themselves. He was now enjoying being the focus of attention and admiration as the story of the exploit began to spread and expand.

The following Sunday morning the Dawley family were up early as usual. Their mother felt that first Mass was the only one worth going to, and everyone in the house had to be up and washed and dressed with their shoes glittering, an hour before it was time to set out. There was nothing Mrs Dawley detested more than people being late for Mass, especially if they were her relatives.

She and her husband walked briskly the two miles to the little church, proud of the healthy children, who walked in a group some distance in front of their parents. They were dignified and careful to salute every woman they met on the road, for they were aware that the eagle eye of their father was watching their every move. He loved his children and was proud of them, but he expected high standards in return.

"We might be poor," he used to say when he had them all together, "but money can't buy either good manners nor good breeding. Make sure you boys lift your cap to every woman you meet, even if she's a beggar. If I hear of you not doing this, you won't lift your cap again for you'll have no head to lift it off."

The family were always among the first worshippers to reach the church. The children marched to their seats at the front where they took their places. The mother quietly selected a spot about half way up the left hand side of the church, for this was the womens' side, and no woman was allowed anywhere else unless she went upstairs to the gallery. There she knelt down to say her rosary before Mass would begin. The father on the other hand joined the group of men who were leaning against the graveyard wall, smoking and chatting. It had long been the custom that the men would gather so, before going into Mass, and it would be a strange man indeed who would break this practice.

At five minutes to the hour an altar boy came out of the vestry and rang a big bell in the yard. This was the signal for the men to begin shuffling slowly into their places in the church, and it was designed by Fr. Nolan to avoid their being late, after he discovered that there was no way he could stop them congregating at the gate. The priest and the altar boys kept a careful eye on the men's progress into the church, and only when it was completed to the priest's satisfaction, would he emerge into the sanctuary to begin Mass.

Fr. Nolan and his boys lined up before the altar as usual, and he ascended the steps to place the covered chalice carefully in front of the tabernacle. Descending the steps again he would turn to face the altar and Mass would begin. But this Sunday, when he came down the steps, Fr. Nolan walked to the sanctuary gate and stood, obviously surveying the lines of children. All eyes were focussed on the priest and on the children before him. Hardly a person in the church dared breathe.

The priest's eyes wandered up and down the rows, and they finally came to rest on young Mick Dawley, where he knelt in the middle of the second row. Now the priest moved slowly forward and, leaning over the front seat and the children in it, he gripped Mick by the lobe of his right ear. In this fashion he drew the boy to a standing position, and then led him along the seat to the middle aisle. Still without a word Mick was led through the sanctuary gate, which was then closed behind them. Fr. Nolan retained his hold and upward pull on the ear, and so led the boy up the steps and to the right hand side of the altar. He carefully positioned him on the very corner of the top platform of the altar so that he faced the congregation.

The priest never said a word but went down the steps, turned to face the altar and his booming voice filled the church as he blessed himself.

"In nomine Patris et Filii it Spiritus Sancti."

The boys mumbled in unison, "Amen."

The Glow of the Oil Lamp

Mick Dawley had not moved and Fr. Nolan ignored him, but the boy knew that the eyes of the entire congregation were on him. He could sense their great curiosity. He carefully avoided looking down the men's side of the church, lest he should catch a glimpse of his father, but out of the corner of his eye he could see his mother praying earnestly at the end of her seat. Even from that distance and without looking directly at her, he was aware that her face was burning red, and there was confusion in her movements as she fingered her beads. He became aware too, of Charlie Madden whispering to his companions, and rubbing his hands in glee, and he sensed that Charlie was gaining a great deal of satisfaction and amusement from this particular act of worship.

The opening prayers, the epistle, the gospel and the offertory, all passed and still Mick maintained his position. Only when the canon of the Mass began, did Fr. Nolan whisper over to him, "Turn round, boy, and kneel down for the Consecration." After the Consecration Mick was told to resume his original position and he remained standing thus until the sermon, which preceded the final blessing.

Fr. Nolan turned to face the people and give his sermon. For a long dramatic moment he allowed his gaze to sweep backwards and forwards so that he had the complete and undivided attention of his flock. Then raising his arms to heaven he spoke slowly and solemnly:

"The text of my sermon today, my dear brethren is, 'Destroy this temple'."

The Glow of the Oil Lamp

There was utter silence as the priest paused for another long, dramatic pause. The fact that the quotation was so short and incomplete was not lost on the majority of the people.

Mick Dawley could feel the priest's eyes and attention turn to him, even though Fr. Nolan was somewhat behind him at the other side of the altar. Out of the corner of his eye he could see the long arm sweep in a wide circle before stopping and pointing directly at him. He tried hard not to see any particular person in the church, but this was difficult due to their apparent proximity. The text brought before his mind the vision of three people struggling in the ruins of a jam wall, and he knew well that that was exactly what it was meant to do.

The priest's extended left arm and pointing finger, riveted the attention of the congregation on the boy. Mick began to squeeze the fingers of one hand with the other as he held them behind his back. For a moment the thought of flight flashed through his mind but the priest was between him and the vestry door, and there was no other route of escape. The sweat began to trickle down his face and he felt almost physically sick. The crowd before his eyes seemed to come and go in a mist, and he thought that for the first time in his life he was going to faint. Again the strong voice of the priest filled the building:

"Behold, my dear brethren, the young man from among our flock, who has taken the Lord's words absolutely to heart." Again there was a long pause and the anticipation of the people was so strong that it could almost be felt in the heavy air. "But, my dear brethren, he has decided to destroy, not the temple in far away Jerusalem, but the homes of the decent people of this parish."

The slow, clipped speech, the startled gasps and the sensation of his own blood pounding in his ears, now seemed to Mick like the rumble of falling masonry. The sermon seemed to go on and on forever, but now the boy was unaware of the actual words. He was in a sick daze and his mind seemed to close out the sounds and their meaning. He felt sick and faint and he had to lean back and seek support from the altar or he would have fallen. At last, however, the priest gave the last blessing and dismissed his people. He told Mick to descend the steps and join the altar boys in their march to the vestry.

The boy wondered what new terrors now lay before him, and he found it hard to stay in line for he felt quite dizzy. He wondered vaguely how he would ever again face his parents, and he dreaded the next meeting with his father. He thought too of the juicy topic of conversation he would provide from one end of the parish to the other.

The vestry door closed with a bang and the priest turned to thank his altar boys. Then, looking into Mick Dawley's eyes, and still holding the covered chalice before him, he said softly, "I hope you have learned a lesson today my boy, that you will never forget for the rest of your life. You must know that the seventh commandment tells us to respect the property of others. I hope I will never again hear your name connected with trouble as long as I am in this parish. Now be off home with you and be sure to pray to God for forgiveness."

"Thank you, Father."

Mick covered the few steps to the outer door with as much eagerness and speed as his weak legs would allow, and he was filled with fear that they would collapse under him. He pressed the latch and pulled the door open, only to find the exit blocked by the broad body of his father.

James Dawley's hand was still raised for he was about to open the door just as it was pulled away from him. Father and son stood facing each other for the floor of the vestry was about a foot higher than the outer step and this meant that Mick's eyes were almost level with his father's. James put his hand on his son's shoulder and stepped to one side of the doorway. Only then was Mick aware that his mother was standing behind her husband.

"Go on home, son, and tell Nellie to get the dinner ready. Hurry on now."

Mick could hardly believe his ears. The tone was gentle and his father had said not a single word about the damage he had caused. The boy passed as quickly as he could between his parents and breathed great gulps of the fresh country air. The altar boys who were still in the passageway, showered him with questions but he hardly heard them. He ignored them and set off for home as fast as he could run.

James Dawley stood aside and allowed his wife to precede him into the vestry. He followed her and they stood side by side before Fr. Nolan, just as he finished devesting. The priest looked up at the couple and said quickly:

"I take it you have come round to apologise for all the damage your son did. I must point out to you, however, that you should not be apologising to me, but to the Raffertys whose house was attacked."

James moved forward half a pace so that he stood very close to the priest. His steel blue eyes looked steadily into Fr. Nolan's brown eyes. " Well, if that's what you think, you've got it all wrong. We did not come round here to apologise to you. That was a damnable thing that you done out there to our lad this morning. I can tell you now that if you were not wearing them clothes and that collar, you wouldn't be worth gathering up when I was finished with you."

Fr. Nolan stepped back in horror. No one had ever questioned anything that he had done before, let alone speak to him like this. Anger blazed in his eyes as he said, "What way is that to speak to a priest of God?"

" I never spoke to a priest like that before and I hope I never will again." James was calm and his words measured. "What you done out there today was a total disgrace and I will not stand up and let you off with it. Why couldn't you have told the whole thing to us in the first place? It is some way to find out what happened when your son is put up in front of the whole parish. A damned disgrace. We might be poor, but I never owed any man anything in my whole life, and I'm damned sure I'm not going to start now. I can deal with my own children without disgracing the whole family in front of the parish. How would you like to be Mick this morning, or me, or Lizzie here?"

Fr. Nolan was silent. He looked at the humble couple before him in their rough Sunday clothes. Then looking down at the floor, and rubbing the toe of his shoe on the oilcloth he said, " Maybe it was a mistake. I hope this won't come between us."

The Dawleys walked home sadly, and in almost total silence. The Sunday dinner was ready and the family ate it quietly. When it was finished James looked round the table and said, "I suppose we'll have to see what we can do to fix up Rafferty's house in the morning."

The incident was never again mentioned in the house within James Dawley's lifetime.

CHAPTER 13
A FEW DAYS MITCHING

Mitching was a pastime, which some pupils in the school turned into an art form. For my own part I only engaged in it on one occasion for a four day period. It was the late spring time and four of us decided to spend our time hiding out in Holmes's planting, which was a small wood about half a mile from the village of Benburb, and just off the road to Blackwatertown. After the first day, when we had explored the entire wood I found the exercise boring. Towards the end of the third day we decided that if we were to camp out correctly, we should cook ourselves a good meal in the middle of the next day. One person was to bring a big saucepan, someone else was to steal a few potatoes, a third was to arrange for a fire, while my job was to get hold of a hen, which we could boil. The only place that I knew of, where I could acquire a convenient hen was Jemmy Dillon's, which was at Blackwatertown. It meant going practically all the way to school, catching the hen, and then coming back to our hiding place.

The next morning I left my schoolbag in the planting and then made my way to Dillon's. Fortunately just as I arrived, Mrs Dillon was finishing feeding the hens, and as she left she called her husband to come in for a cup of tea. As they disappeared into the house all the hens were busily pecking away at the corn, which had been thrown down for them in the yard. I crawled through an opening in the hedge, made my way carefully over towards the hens and grabbed one by the leg. Before she could make a sound, I used my free hand to cover her mouth. I was used to working with hens, and taking advantage of a barrel, which happened to be sitting there, to hide me from them, I crawled up to them, and the others did not notice.

Quietly I bent the hen's head under her wing, rocked her gently to and fro for a minute or two and she lay sleeping in my arms. Carefully I made my way out through the hedge and using the old road, which ran parallel to the new one and was very quiet, made my way back to the planting. There I found my three companions all ready to start getting the midday meal ready.

The first job was to kill the hen. We all knew that one held a hen by the legs and pulled her neck and she would die easily. Each of us tried to accomplish this feat in turn but the hen obstinately refused to relinquish life. In fact the more we pulled at her neck, the more alive she seemed to become, and she began to squalk and make a terrible noise. Even though we were a good distance from human habitation, it seemed a miracle that someone's attention had not been attracted by the din. Having totally failed to kill the hen by the normal method we decided to hang her to a branch of a tree and cut her throat. This presented a problem in that we only had one knife, and that was so blunt that it failed to make any impression on the bird's neck. At this point we decided to pluck the hen, since I knew that it was easier to pull the feathers out while she was still warm. The problem of killing her was left in abeyance.

The hen was almost plucked, and our clearing was covered with feathers when we heard someone approaching through the woods. But for the fact that he was calling his dog, we might not have heard him at all, and he would have caught us red handed. I tried to move the hen so that she would be better hidden, but in so doing I must have loosened the string and the bird fell to the ground. With a great squalk and flurry of wings, she went flying across the clearing in a desperate bid for freedom. We all dived into a clump of whins and lay on our tummies waiting to see who the intruder was. To our great surprise the sergeant of the police appeared in ordinary clothes with a big yellow Labrador dog walking at heel, and a gun over his arm. The policeman stood in the clearing with his dog sitting at heel, and gazing through the trees in the direction in which our dinner had disappeared. I hardly dared breathe for dogs always came to me, and I was sure that this one would do the same. The sergeant took off his cap, scratched his head, looked at all the feathers and said, "Well, that's the best ever I've seen in my life. A fox must have caught the hen and was about to eat her. I think, Tinker, we just deprived him of his dinner."

The sergeant seemed to stand there for ages. But at last he looked at the sitting dog and said, "Heel Tinker.

I'm on duty in half an hour. We'd better make our way home, boy." The sergeant turned towards the village and disappeared through the trees. We lay silent for a long time and then crawled out into the clearing. Our final day of mitching had turned into somewhat of a failure, but at least we had not been caught. It was a pastime that I never attempted again.

Monday of the next week meant going back to school and I was relieved. One of the boys who had been mitching, had a cousin at secondary school in Dungannon, and he arranged with him, that he would get four good notes written for Mr. Colgan to cover our absence. We had to pay a shilling each for this valuable service.

We went into school and presented our notes. The master hardly glanced at them, but threw them into the drawer of his desk and went on with lessons. At the end of the day, however, he told the other three to get their parents to write longer notes, as he needed these for the inspector. They had missed quite a few days and the inspector would demand long letters to explain the four day absence. I was kept behind to sweep the floor, but I could see that the other three had long and worried faces.

I swept the floor and went to lift my bag to go home. Mr. Colgan sat looking at me and then he said, " I was thinking that it would be a good idea if you called into Dillons this evening, and told Mrs Dillon how sorry you are for stealing her hen, and scaring the rest of them. Since your mother has hens at home, I'm surprised that you took a hen that did not belong to you. I would have thought that it would have been easier to leave your books hidden, and push a hen of your own into the bag. Or maybe you thought your mother could not afford a hen and Mrs Dillon could. And by the way I wonder what your mother would say if you started plucking her hens while they are still alive. I am disappointed that you have not more feeling for other creatures than to do the likes of that to any bird or animal."

He sat in his usual place looking at me. He did not seem angry or annoyed, and there was an air of slight amusement about him. I wondered how he had got to know what we had done, and that worried me. I looked back at him, and could not think of anything to say that would make any sense, and I was wondering how I could get word to the other boys that they did not need notes, even if they could get some. I looked down at the floor and felt really uncomfortable.

"What did you intend doing with the hen?," the master asked.

"We intended to boil her and make a dinner out of her, Sir."

"And what else were you having for the dinner?"

"Potatoes Sir."

"So it was going to be a sort of feast was it? That would have been right and tasty."

I could see that he was now quite amused and was finding it hard not to laugh. I did not know what to say and I was not sure he wished me to say anything. He knew all he needed to know. He looked at me and smiled, "Now I'm giving you a note for your mother. It asks her not to send you to school until half past ten tomorrow. I have made some daft excuse to satisfy her. But I do not want you meeting the others, and this will avoid you doing so. I think you will have had your fill of mitching, and I can't see you doing it again. Now call with Mrs Dillon on the way home."

I was dreading calling at Dillons, but I had no alternative. Mrs Dillon welcomed me with a big smile, and when I told her what I had done she went into fits of laughter. She went and got me some chocolate from a drawer, and told me to go on home and leave the hens alone in the future. Thanks to Mrs Dillon's good nature, it was certainly not as bad an experience as I had anticipated.

I arrived into school an hour late the next day to find my three companions lined up under the clock and looking very sorry for themselves. They had failed to produce notes and had given all sorts of crazy excuses. The master had led them on a wild goose chase and had then given them a good beating. No one could understand why I was late, and I did not enlighten them. Mr. Colgan was right, I never tried mitching again.

Benburb village in 1947. James Bruce has a wall built to separate the village from his mansion and give him privacy.

CHAPTER 14
A WEE BIT OF A SHAKING

Many people believed that when the twelfth of July came around, there was bound to be a spell of good weather. The Orangemen attributed this phenomenon to the fact that God always looks after his own, whereas nationalists tended to think that the blessing originated from a totally different source. Normally the whole country closed down for a holiday of at least a week. Protestant people saw this as a reasonable way to celebrate their victory at the Battle of the Boyne, and Catholics had to go along with it. At that time, in the surrounding towns, almost all the shops were owned by Protestants, and this greatly restricted what people could do. It was a very strange Protestant indeed who would not go to the twelfth celebration, or who would work normally during the few days around the twelfth.

Joe Allen, however, did not mind being seen as strange at all, and saw the prospect of good weather as an ideal time to get a lot of work done. A few days before the twelfth one year, he came over to our house to ask my father to cut the hay for him on the holiday, as he had no one who could handle the horses. My father was on night shift at the time and the mill was one of the very few places, which stayed open. He told Joe that if he could get a couple of hours sleep, he would give him a day or two, but he'd be starting late.

On the morning of the twelfth the countryside resounded to the sound of Lambeg drums, and quite early in the morning bands could be heard in the distance as they made their way to the meeting points. It was the outward sign of deep enjoyment and satisfaction felt by the participants, and of deep resentment felt by most Catholics, and this is exactly how it was meant to be. About ten o'clock my father appeared after only three hours sleep, and having got a cup of tea, he told me to come along with him for a day's work at Allen's. "I might need you to drive the horses out to the fields, and to bring them back in the evening," he said, as though this were imposing a heavy burden on me. "And then when we break off for something to eat in the middle of the day, you will have to ride one of the horses home to let him get a bite of corn. I couldn't handle the two horses on my own, all the way round the road." Needless to say he did not have to coax me, once I heard about working with the horses.

We arrived at Allen's and Joe was busy sharpening the blades of the mowing machine, or as he called them the fingers. My father took over this job immediately and it was obvious that he thought Joe was not a great hand at the sharpening. Mrs Allen was busy about the house, and as usual she asked me to feed the hens and see to the wee turkeys. She had not been well for quite a while, and my mother sent me over most days after school with an apple tart or a bannock of soda bread. Although the Allens were very rich, they lived as though they had nothing at all, and worked every minute possible. Joe always judged a person's worth by the amount of money or land he left when he died. Mrs Allen would never offer any money but my mother said a good turn was never wasted. I had to give a hand nearly every day so I knew exactly what was wanted. I could not wait, however, to get working with the horses.

I had a really fantastic day that day for my father let me sit on one of the seats of the mowing machine, and allowed me to hold the reins nearly all the time. The only time he needed to interfere was when we were turning at the headrig and footrig, and even then he let me do most of the task myself, quietly guiding me as to how I could get complete control. At teatime he loosed the horses out of the machine and put me up on one's back, to ride it back to the house. He walked between the two horses, holding their bridles, and I rode like a king on my horse behind him. It was a day I would dream of for many years to come. I was allowed to ride the horse back again after tea, and to take the reins once more when we got back to work.

We cut three fields of hay that day, and in the evening we ended up in a meadow, which Joe had beside the lough. It was after eight o'clock in the evening when we finished it, and this time I had to drive the horses home, still harnessed to the mowing machine. Joe had been cutting the grass round the edges of the meadow with a scythe, and we left him there, for he still had a little more to do. It was more than half a mile back to the

The Glow of the Oil Lamp

house, and I was very proud when we met two or three neighbours on the road, and they saw me in charge of the horses.

We drove the horses into the yard and across the front of the byre to an area where Joe usually kept the machine. Suddenly Da gave a shout, "Hold the horses there, boy, for a minute or two, and watch what's going on up there at the dairy." The dairy was up to the left, but he jumped off the machine and ran to the byre door, which was on our right. I was puzzled because there was nothing going on at the dairy, and after a second or two, I looked to the right to see where Da had gone. By the time I looked in his direction he was putting a jacket over Mrs Allen's body, for she was lying dead in the byre door, between two full buckets of milk.

My father walked over and held the horses' heads. "Run as hard as you can, Son," he said, "and tell Joe to get back here as quickly as he can. Tell him I need his help to loose out the horses. Don't tell him anything else. Now go as fast as you can."

This time I went across the fields, and I ran as if my life depended on it. When I got back to the meadow Joe had only about fifty yards of grass left to cut. I ran up to him and panted, "Come on back quickly Joe, Da needs you. He needs you now. Come on Joe as fast as you can go."

Joe looked at me in amazement and shook his head. "Troth and sang, boy, what is wrong with you? Sure your Da could handle twenty horses and there's only two. I'll finish cutting this wee bit of grass."

The Glow of the Oil Lamp

I pulled at Joe's shirt, which was hanging over his trousers. "Come on now Joe, and don't mind the grass. Da needs you. Come on Joe, please come on Joe. We're taking far too much time and Da will be angry."

Joe looked at me in total bewilderment and rubbed one hand through his hair, leaving the scythe against the hedge with the other. "Troth and sang, lad, I can't understand what is wrong with you at all. Anybody would think that half the world is dead, to see you in this state. Come on, and we'll see what's wrong. Troth and sang I never saw a lad in such a state over nothing."

As we made our way back across the fields, I could not get Joe to come quickly enough, and I kept urging him to walk a wee bit harder. He was perplexed because most evenings he and I would be walking about together and I had never behaved like this before. In spite of my distress I was determined not to tell him what had happened and to obey my father's command. We got to the house and Da came out on to the street from the byre. He walked up to Joe and put his hand on his shoulder. "Joe," he said quietly, "There's bad news. Mrs Allen has had a turn. She's down here by the byre. I'm sorry Joe but the news is not good. Come on down here and see for yourself."

The two men turned and made their way towards the byre and I started to go along with them. Da stopped and pointed up the lane. "Go on home now, Arthur," he said firmly, "Go home and tell your mother what has happened and ask her to make a few bannocks of bread if she can. And tell her that a couple of apple tarts would be useful if she can get any apples. Tell her I'll be home after a while but not to wait up for me if I am a bit late. Go on now like a good lad, get the cow milked and fed and get to bed as soon as you can."

I had no option but to do what I was told, although I would have liked to stay and see all that was going on. I told my mother what had happened and what Da had said, and she was shocked. "You'll have to say a few prayers for her tonight," she said. "The poor craytur must never have had a chance to make peace with her Lord. She was a good craytur too and I am sure she's in heaven. But say a prayer for her anyway before you go to bed. I have enough stuff to make a couple of bannocks of bread but I haven't many apples. It's hard to get good apples at this time of the year and your father should know that. Sometimes I believe that man thinks that I am a magician. Go and do your work and then get ready for bed."

I lay and tossed and tumbled for a long time. I did not want to go to sleep for I wanted to hear what Da would have to say when he got home. It was the first time in my life that I was near to someone when they died, and I was excited and a little afraid. I was drifting off to sleep when I heard the door slam shut, and then my father talking to my mother.

"Och dammit, Sarah, are you not in bed? Why didn't you go on to bed and not bother waiting up for me? I came home when a crowd of people gathered in and Joe's brothers and sister arrived. Och dammit Sarah, I found the poor craytur lying in the byre door and her with two full buckets of milk. When Joe got back he looked at her and he said that it was a tarra that she fell dead and never spilled a drop of the milk. He said she was as good a worker as ever he had seen in his life. That seems to be all he thinks of, but the whole thing hasn't hit him yet. When he said that about the milk I couldn't help thinking of how his brother had been drowned in the lough nearly forty years ago. The father came down from the county Armagh and looked at him laid out in the meadow, and said, 'Would you look at him lying there and a whole lifetime's work left in him.' Come on now and we'll have a drop of tea and get to bed. We'll have to go over there tomorrow and see what needs to be done." They must have sat down at the fire at this point and their voices became quite indistinct. My eyes were getting very heavy and soon I drifted off to sleep.

The next day my parents went over to Allen's quite a number of times, but they would not allow me near the place, even to help with the hens or turkeys. The day after that was the funeral, which took place in the afternoon, and Da took me with him for he said I needed to pay my respects. It was the first funeral I had ever attended, and it was a Protestant funeral into the bargain. The rules of the Catholic Church decreed that Catholics could follow the cortege, but they were not allowed to enter the church. When we reached the church, however, Da took me by the hand and led me inside as though this were the normal thing to do. A couple of other Catholics came in too, but the vast majority stopped at the door, and waited outside to join the funeral on its way to the graveyard.

My father did not pay too much attention to rules that he did not agree with. He had a great habit of saying, "I can't see any sense in that and I'm damned if I'm going to do it, no matter what they say." His independence had been made stronger when his younger brother had died of diphtheria and his coffin was not allowed into the church in the Moy, even though it was in a special coffin. It had to sit on trestles in the yard in front of the door while the Mass was being said. Da took serious objection to this, and he said that if they could not let his brother enter the chapel, then he would not enter it either. I do not know who had refused permission, and it may well have been the health authorities. For some years afterwards, however, he would not go to Mass except to attend a funeral. This state of affairs greatly annoyed my mother, and she said that there could not be luck in a house where there was someone who did not attend Mass. Eventually he gave in and went every Sunday as normal.

After the service in the church, we followed the hearse down to the graveyard and there was another service there. We paid our respects to Joe and walked home, which was only half a mile away. That, however, was not the end of Da's connection with the funeral.

One man in the area claimed to be very religious, and to be a first class Catholic. I discovered from the talk of our visitors in the house, that for some time this man had been teasing Da about his attendance at Protestant funerals and casting up to him, that for some years he had not gone to Mass at all. Apparently Da ignored him and said that the auld eejet was not worth bothering about.

At that time Da took a shortcut through the grounds of the manor house to get to his work. Strictly speaking this was forbidden but no one paid any attention, and it saved a journey of some three miles on the bicycle. A couple of days after the Allen funeral, having walked through the grounds, Da came to the white bridge, which had been erected many years before by James Bruce, and which spans the river Blackwater. The exemplary Catholic gentleman was on the bridge and coming in the opposite direction. Coming within earshot he started to speak loudly as though talking to a companion.

"There's some quare fine Protestants about here that think they are Catholics. It takes a great Catholic to go to the Protestant church for a service. It's a wonder Dawley that you don't go to the Protestant church on a Sunday, and leave the chapel clean for decent Catholic people."

By this time he was level with Da and sneering into his face. Da sprang suddenly and grabbed him by the back of the neck and the seat of his pants and lifted him over the railing of the bridge and held him there, fifteen feet above the steaming waters below, for the river was in flood. There were quite a few people along the banks that evening as it had been a lovely day, and they witnessed the entire incident as it unfolded.

Holding him now by the back of his jacket Da pushed him forward so that he was hanging upside down. "Maybe you'd like to go and meet your maker this evening, since your such a great friend of his," he growled. "It's not too often I get a chance of drowning something that badly needs to be drowned. You were right and lucky that you were born in a dry year, for anybody that would keep you, would drown nothing."

"Oh for God's sake pull me back, Mick," the man pleaded in a terrified voice. "I didn't mean any harm and you won't hear anything from me any more. Pull me back, Mick, for God's sake."

"It's a wonder the likes of you can be so nice to an auld Protestant like me," sneered my father giving him a further jerk forward. "Shout down to those people down there that you are a rotten auld hypocrite, and that there's not a decent bone in your body."

"I'm a rotten hypocrite, and I haven't a decent bone in my body," shouted the man in obvious agony.

"That's not near loud enough," said Da, "Bawl it out there so that all the people along the banks can hear your confession. They say confession is powerful good for your soul."

The man used every ounce of energy he had in his body to obey the command, and was greeted by roars of laughter from below. Da still held him in the same position.

"Now tell them that never again will you interfere with people going about their business."

Again the gentleman put all his efforts into doing exactly what he was told. Da pulled him back and turning him round held him against the railings of the bridge. He was clearly terrified and badly shaken.

"Och now Mick," he groaned, "I'm sorry for annoying you and getting involved in your business but I didn't mean any harm. I never realised that you were as strong as a bull. You have me nearly killed. I hoped to get you to see that you should obey the laws of our church. That's all I wanted. I'm sorry."

"Don't you dare start preaching at me," roared Da, going red in the face and shaking the man like a rat. "Only I don't want to dirty my hands I'd plaster your face all over those railings. The only reason that you are a Catholic is that you were born one, and you have never thought about what you're doing in your life. So never you dare preach at me. There's more brains in the head of a brush than there is in that head of yours. Now go on home and behave yourself, for if ever I have to chastise you again, I'll kill you stone dead."

And so it was that Mrs Allen's death ended in a confrontation on the bridge. Everyone said that Da had done the right thing, and that the man had it all coming for a long time. It was remarked afterwards that if he saw Da in the distance he would turn and go the other way or travel miles out of his way to avoid him. Da's version of the incident was, "I only gave him a wee bit of a shaking."

CHAPTER 15
THE TALE OF A ROANEY COW

I was very young when my father started giving me a set of jobs to do every morning and evening. They were all to do with cattle and I loved cattle, and I loved working with them and took a pride in it. I think I was not much more than six when it started, and at the time my father had a job targing toe in Benburb. This was part of the process of cleaning flax and it was a very dangerous occupation, but compared to other jobs there was great money for it. My father was very dexterous at it and could earn the best wages in the factory. Sometimes he worked the night shift, and at other times he went out at five o'clock in the morning, and so he expected me to look after the cattle for him.

We usually had two cows and for a couple of years we had three. Each morning I had to make sure that the cows had hay, which had to be brought from a stack in the top field, which was about a hundred yards away. My father taught me how to pull the hay from the stack so that it was tidy and then to make it into a bottle. A bottle was made by pulling as much hay as one could hold against one's tummy, and then making hay ropes by pulling and twisting two thin lines of hay by hand from the bundle, so that they protruded like two tails. These ropes were then wound round the bundle in opposite directions and fastened together. Only then could one drop the bottle, which would stay neatly together and could be easily carried. I was very proud of my ability to make bottles of hay for my father always gave me great praise for the work I did.

As well as the hay the cows had to get a little meal every morning in a bucket. I took great pleasure in giving them the meal and seeing them enjoying it while I milked them into a big white enamel bucket. This was all man's work and I loved it. In the evening after school I had to clean out the byre, and wheel away the manure in a small barrow, which my father had made me for the job. Then I had to bed the cows with straw, and put some straw into the group where the dung fell so that everything in the byre was spotless. My father inspected the byre every few days and he never failed to praise me for the work I had done so well. On a Saturday he always gave me a half crown, for he said that a man needed his wages at the end of the week.

I must have been about eight when my father brought home the roaney cow. We already had a blue cow, Daisy, but we needed milk when she was dry. I could milk Daisy without any bother at all and she had a daughter, a heifer called Molly, which was not any bother either. But the roaney cow proved to be another story. I gave her the hay and milk just like Daisy. She stood in her stall and chewed contentedly, and when I sat down at her right side to milk her, she did not kick

The Glow of the Oil Lamp

nor move. But she had a habit of dunging down her tail while she was being milked, and then she would swing the tail so that no matter how I watched, she could catch me round the neck with it and I ended up plastered. I told our neighbour, Barney Conlon about the problem and he explained that it was a sign of friendship, a kind of 'thank you' for the hay and milk. I did not see it as a very friendly gesture at all, and when my father advised me to tie her tail to a post before I started, I thought the problem was solved.

But the second problem was even more difficult. Every time I got the bucket full of lovely warm milk she would lift her foot and plant it right in the middle of it. Since she had already dunged down the leg the milk had to be used for feeding wee calves. My father got me a strong rope to tie her leg to the bottom of a post, but no matter what I did she still managed to get a foot into the milk in spite of me. One Saturday morning my father got me up early so that he could show me how to milk the roaney cow.

He gave her hay and meal just like I did. He rubbed her all over and he talked to her. Then he carefully tied the tail and the foot to the post, and sat down on the stool to milk her. He was so happy that he had things under full control, that he sang his favourite song, the Sessiagh Hare while he was milking. He got the big white bucket filled to the brim and looking at me with a satisfied smile he said, "I can't understand, Boy, why you have any bother milking that cow. She's as quiet as a lamb, and she's the best milking cow ever I seen in my life."

The Glow of the Oil Lamp

He got up and put his stool to one side. He took his bucket of milk and was walking past me to the door of the byre with a very satisfied smile on his face and singing away contentedly to himself. Standing on the tied leg, the cow let fly with the other leg just when he was in the right place. She drove my father and his bucket of milk out through the door of the byre, and about ten yards down the garden. He ended up lying in a heap covered with milk and dirt. His thigh hurt where she hit him, but obviously his pride hurt even more. I did not wish to see my father hurt, but I had to turn my face into the corner of the byre to laugh. I could have hugged the roaney cow.

That was the one time in my life that I ever saw my father nearly abuse an animal. He got a big stick, and was about to beat her when my mother rushed in between him and her, and forced him to stop. "For God's sake, Mick, are you off in the head? She's only a dumb animal. You'll have to beat me too if you want to hit her."

"That bloody cow could have killed the cub, and it would have been my fault, Sarah.

I can tell you now, there's no way any ordinary man could milk that animal. She'll have to go to the next Moy fair. God, she could have killed the child; she damned near killed me."

My father was red in the face. He was angry and embarrassed. My mother took him by the hand and led him into the house to get a cup of tea. I put my arms round the neck of the roaney cow. I felt it was my fault that she had got into trouble and would have to go. She licked my hand with her big rough tongue.

On Monday morning when I was doing my work my mother came into the byre. Gently she tied a rope round the cow's neck, looped her tail into it, and then tied each foot to a post. "See if you can milk her now, Son," she said, for milking a cow was one of the skills that my mother could never master, hard though she tried. I filled the big bucket with milk and carried it out. The cow never moved. We did the same thing twice each day till the end of the week. My mother showed my father the big crock of cream, ready for churning. "Well that beats Bannagher and Bannagher beats the devil," he said, "I was going to sell her but she is too good a cow to let go if we can help it. Are you sure she's safe?"

"Oh I know now how to handle her, Da," I said with great pride and satisfaction. "She's as quiet as a lamb and I don't even have to touch her."

My father looked at me and said nothing. He walked out to the front door and stood on the doorstep, whistling to himself and looking all round the countryside. Then he came in and looked at me. "It's a good man that knows when he's wrong," he said quietly. "It's a far better one that admits it, and that's a lesson that I hope you'll remember for the rest of your life."

I never forgot the roaney cow and I hope I never forget the lesson.

My mother loved making butter and was proud of her skill at it and of the care she took in scalding all the utensils used in the butter making. But she was not so good at the churning. I think that was because she was too small for the big barrel churn with its long handled dash. So one day each week when I came home from school it was my job to do the churning. I stood on a chair at the side of the churn and kept the dash going up and down for three quarters of an hour or so. While I was doing this, my mother would tell me stories of her youth in Glasgow, and sometimes sing the old Scottish songs that her mother had taught her as a girl. She had a good voice and was quite musical, a gift which I did not inherit, unfortunately. When she thought the milk was almost churned she would stop me and open the churn. "That butter's just about ready to break," she would say, "Another five or ten minutes will finish it." It was a fairly heavy job but for some reason I always enjoyed it. Perhaps it was because my mother kept talking all the time, and I got a clear picture of the young city girl in my imagination.

As far as I can remember it was that same year that my father made two hen arks. That was before the deep litter came in, and the hens were kept in small arks in the field or garden. Each ark was about six feet high with a pitched tin roof. The floor was about ten feet long and six wide and there were laying boxes down each side of the house. My father involved me in each step of the process and I think it gave me an interest in woodwork that has lasted for the rest of my life. "The roofs of these henhouses have to be painted," he said to me when he had the job finished. " I got a tin of red paint up in Boyd's shop in Benburb and a fine big brush, and I want you to do the job. I'll inspect it on Saturday when I expect you to have it finished, and I'll expect to see a couple of the finest arks in the country."

The next day at school was the longest any human being ever spent. I had no interest in what was going on; I could not wait to get home to get started to the painting and my mother could hardly get me to eat any dinner. It took me the rest of the evenings of the week to do the job, and I heard my mother telling Mrs Conlon that I had all about the house painted red, as well as the henhouses, and that she had better watch out or their place would be painted as well. "That Mick has no sense at all," she said, "he could have had the job done himself in an hour, and he has the child covered in paint all week. There's not a stitch left about the place that has not been stained with paint from the lad's hands or clothes."

"That's as fine a bit of painting as ever any man saw," said my father on Saturday. That was all I wanted to hear, for what would women know about that kind of thing anyway?

Julia Jordan (nee Daly) with her son, Tommy, taken about 1943/4. Tommy is about seven years old.

CHAPTER 16
THE ROAD TO THE FAIR

A man told me lately that he has a friend who is addicted to cattle. I think I understood what he meant, for although we only had three or four at any one time, I loved them. Wee calves, big calves or cows, it was all the same. I enjoyed feeding them, cleaning out their houses, watching them grazing, or lying amongst them in the field as they lay in a ring, chewing their cuds, on a sunny summer day. Most of all I loved gazing into those big, deep, gentle eyes and wondering what they were thinking about. There always seemed to be a wealth of wisdom in those deep orbs that man would never understand. But maybe a child could! At least he could imagine a world where wealth and effort had no meaning.

It was never possible to get real affection from them like it was with the dog or even a goat. But nevertheless, I always felt close to them, and that closeness is one of the lasting and dearest memories of my childhood. We shared an innocence, a gentleness, and a total dependence on others, that those not reared in the country could ever hope to understand. It was always a source of sadness, therefore, when my father decided that it was time for some of my friends to depart, or rather be taken away. And from about the age of seven years onwards, I was the one who had to lead them on their final journey.

It was just over four miles from our house to the famous fair in the Moy. Three of those miles were over narrow country lanes, which turned and twisted and were lined with gaps and other openings. The gaps, or other escape routes were the real reason for my presence. In each one I had to stand to prevent the cattle from straying into roadside fields. The trick was to stand in the gap in such a way that one could immediately run in front of the cattle again, as soon as they had passed the danger point, and be ready for action at the next place of danger.

After some two and a half miles we reached a place called Shield's road, from which our house was visible, only a few hundred yards away across the fields. We had come in almost a full circle, right round the great hill, which is topped by Sessiagh fort. It always seemed to me a great pity that there was no road across those few fields. By that time I had stood in a hundred gaps and as each was passed, usually managed to get back safely in front of the cattle again. Normally I was pretty agile and was able to block the cattle and get ahead of them again without much bother. But on the odd occasion when I made a mistake, or the cattle evaded me, my father tended to express his annoyance and anger at my stupidity in pretty colourful language. He was known to have a command of meaningful expletives, which was the envy of many who fancied their own talent in this regard.

At each farmhouse along the way, the woman of the house, or less frequently the man, would close wayside gates or stand in gaps, telling me to go on ahead to the next one. "Good boy yourself there. It's a great man you are. What would your Da do without you at all, at all? God, Mick but that's a great bit of a lad you have there altogether, Mick. He's as good as any grown man. I hope you remember to treat him well in the Moy today."

Even if I was just after making a blunder, my father would fully concur, and add words of praise of his own. It all made me feel like a very important cog in a magnificent wheel for my father always made sure that I could hear his answer. "Och, indeed you're right there Joe. He's a powerful man with the cattle altogether, and he's as swift as a hare on his feet. You wouldn't believe the way he can get past the cattle all the time, even when you'd think that they were going to beat him. He seems to know every move they're going to make. Hold them calves where they are there, for a minute or two, Boy."

This, I knew, was the prelude to a longish conversation with the neighbour about the news of the countryside, about the price of cattle, about the likely sort of trade there would be at the fair, about how the war was going, and a thousand other things that might crop up. Finally, as though someone had prodded him with a pitchfork on the behind, there would be the shouted order, "Let them on ahead there boy, or we'll never be in the Moy today. It must have taken us an hour and a half to cover the last mile of ground." He always managed to make it sound as though it had been me who had been doing all the talking and who had held things up.

After three miles or more we reached the Rector's brae where the gravelled lane ran down to the tarred road. One had to be extra careful here for other herders were likely to be on the 'low road', and it was important that groups of cattle did not get mixed up. The sight of strange beasts was inclined to make normally placid cattle go crazy, and so it was necessary to make sure that they were kept well apart. But there were fewer gaps now although one had to make sure to reach the lanes, which led down onto the road before the cattle did. Failure to do so was liable to drive my father crazier than ever the cattle could be. Soon it was just over a mile to the Moy and the village on a low hill was now in sight.

The Moy fair was held on the first Friday of every month. Apparently this had been the case since an old landlord called Lord Charlemont, had ordered one of his servants to sell horses for him on that day each month. The order had been given just before he went on the grand tour in the 1740s. It had originally been mainly a horse fair, but by the time I knew it, at least ninety per cent of the animals were cattle with a few horses, donkeys and ponies confined to the western side of the square. Old men told me that dealers had sold horses to the Greek government during the First World War. The government they had been dealing with was overthrown, and the people who came to power, refused to pay the money owed. Many rich and

The Glow of the Oil Lamp

well known horse dealers from all around the Moy were ruined. Some had spent a lifetime in the courts trying to get their money back. Men loved to tell this story to youngsters like me, so one heard it two or three times every fair day.

The square is probably three hundred yards long and well over a hundred wide and on a fair day it was a hive of intense activity. Dealers were everywhere, shouting, slapping hands, examining beasts, marching angrily away from each other and then, apparently reluctantly, coming back to continue the bargaining. There were men running with ponies and horses to show how strong and fit the animals were; there were trick of the loop men with their stalls; there were all sorts of tricksters who performed all sorts of impossible tasks. One man who never failed to amaze me, invited people to bind him up with chains, lock the chains with huge padlocks, put him in a big sack, and then tie the neck of the sack with a rope. He always escaped in about two minutes and was greeted with a great cheer.

Music too was sometimes part of the scene. There were fiddlers in corners here and there and the odd man with an accordion. Some of the musicians had companions, who sang wonderful old songs, their beauty sometimes lost in the noise and melee around them. Some had song sheets, which they sold for a couple of pennies each. One elderly man with a huge grey beard, which reached to his knees, always sat on a box with a white stick and a dog. I was interested in the big brown and white dog. The man told me one day that the dog was a Saint Bernard, and that he had saved hundreds of lives in the high mountains of Canada. He said the dog should have a barrel of whiskey strapped to his neck, but it was not needed in this country, and anyway, he was too poor to buy such a thing. The man played a harp and had a notice, which said that he was the last of the great, blind, Irish harpers.

After my father sold the cattle, he usually went to the pub, and I was given a shilling or one and sixpence, to get some tea and scones or maybe sweets. The village of the Moy on a fair day was famous for its eating houses. There was a grand hotel in the centre of the western side of the square, but only the ' big hands' ever went there. I never managed to meet anyone who was of sufficient status to dine in the hotel. Mrs White's and Rosie Shield's tea rooms always did a roaring trade. They vied with each other. They were ordinary houses, the front rooms of which had been set with tables and chairs. The farmers did a lot of bargaining about the price of meals, although it was generally reckoned that these were quite reasonable. Sometimes it took as long to bargain about a meal, as it did to buy or sell a calf. The meals were a source of contention among our people. At that time it was forbidden by the Catholic Church to eat flesh meat on a Friday. Protestant neighbours took a special delight in ordering a fine dinner with plenty of meat, and then going out of their way to show how much they were enjoying it. The only consolation for their Catholic neighbours, was that there was a general assurance that they would pay up for their indulgence in the next world. But that was little solace to a hungry man after a whole morning at the fair.

One day while I was waiting for my father, I wandered into a quiet place called the brickrow. I found the great, blind harper sitting in a doorway reading the paper. He explained to me that the blindness only affected him when he took up the harp. With that he got up and looked at the village clock, which was about three hundred yards away. "Be God, Sponger," he said, "It's nearly two o'clock and it's time we were getting back to work. Come on Sponger." Lifting his white stick he started tapping the edge of the walls on his way back to the square, with the faithful Sponger walking slightly ahead of him. It seemed as though the dog was guiding the man.

Coming from our house we always entered the square from the west. The entire eastern side of the huge area was thronged with cattle and dealers, and was a very exciting, if somewhat dangerous place. We always made our way down the main street between the two sections of the square, and turned into Killyman Street, which was also crowded with animals and men. Some two hundred yards or more down that street was the grader. That was our objective. Cattle for sale in the rest of the fair were stores, which needed to be kept for a few more weeks or months before they were ready for killing. My father, however, always finished the cattle and brought them to the grader where they fetched the best prices. He prided himself on having the best cattle in the fair and getting the top prices. To me it was a place of excitement tinged with sadness, for it was where I would say my final farewell to my friends.

The Glow of the Oil Lamp

The main part of the grader was one room of a tiny, tin roofed house, occupied by an old woman. At least at that time she looked old to me, but then to a child everyone who is adult, looks pretty old. On the fair day the room was taken over by two men from the ministry, who weighed and judged the cattle and wrote out the cheques for the accepted beasts. To me they seemed to be men of great power, somewhat like the headmaster in the school, or the priest on the altar. A lot depended on their decisions for money was badly needed. Apart from anything else they were dressed like toffs. At any rate I thought that was how toffs would be dressed. Sometimes the woman would serve them mugs of tea and steaming pancakes. It seemed to me that all the men in the room watched them eat, almost in awe. Maybe they were anxious not to insult these men of power, or maybe it was simply rural shyness.

Outside the side window of the room was a 'bridge', a weighbridge, surrounded by railings. The cattle were driven on to this one by one, and their weight turned the hand of a huge circular clock-like structure, which stood in one corner of the room. It seems probable that particular room was only used on a fair day, for the equipment was certainly permanent. I was always afraid of our cattle not reaching the required mark, but in all the years that I accompanied my father to the fair, that never happened. It was said that Mick Dawley could judge a calf's weight to the last pound, and it was not uncommon for men to ask him advice before bringing cattle to the grader. If Da was in a crooked mood, and he was renowned far and wide for his crookedness, his answer would be like that of the oracle at Delphi, almost impossible to interpret correctly. To ordinary poor men he was always straight, but if he reckoned he was dealing with a 'smart fellow', the answer was unintelligible.

In our school getting off for the fair was a mark of distinction. This was very deeply felt because all children who went to the Moy school, got a special holiday every fair day. The school was closed. Since the Moy was the other side of our parish, this arrangement was deeply resented in our school and most especially by those who had no connection with the land and, therefore, never got a chance of going to the fair. The closure was probably done for safety reasons for it would have been almost impossible for children to make their way through the village on a fair day. I am not sure if the Moy children had to make up for the day off at other times, but this possibility never even occurred to us. It was simply a source of deep envy and resentment. Thus it was taken for granted that if you met a Moy boy, and he was not a complete giant, you were a cissy if you failed to give him a bloody nose, or at least got one yourself in trying.

One time when we had no cattle ready for the fair, my father took me aside on a Wednesday night. As was his usual practice he sat in his chair and we had a boxing match. He would show me how to feint, to punch with all my weight, to use footwork, and to avoid punches. Most of all he took great pains to see that I learned to block punches or to duck out of their way. Sometimes he would allow me to hit him and pretend to be really hurt. And sometimes he would give me a good whack, just to teach me not to be over confident. Finally on this particular night he said that I had tired him out, and he made me sit on a stool in front of him. He looked me straight in the eye. "Now Arthur," he said, "I am going to ask you to do something that I don't like asking. It's not right. If you want, you can refuse to do it but I am going to ask you anyway. James Mulligan has seven calves to go to the fair on Friday. He can't get any help and I can't get off work this week, but he said a lad would do. Unless you really want to go to school, would you ask Mr.Colgan for permission to stay off on Friday? Tell him that I said I am really sorry about this, and it won't happen again."

I could hardly believe my ears. To be asked to go to the fair with our own cattle was a great treat. To be asked to go with a neighbour's was nothing short of a miracle. But it suddenly struck me that it would not be very good policy to let my father see my utter joy and excitement. And I knew it would be total disaster if my mother saw it. I did my best to look a wee bit downcast. "There's been great things going on in the school this last while Da," was all I could think of saying, "but I'll ask Colgan in the morning anyway. Sure it's only one day."

My father looked at me. His face was stern and there was a hard glint in his eye. I knew that I had put my foot in it. "As long as ever you are about this house or talking to me boy, never let me hear you refer to Mr. Colgan except by his proper title." He spat out the words with venom. "And his proper title is Mr. Colgan and I never want to hear you refer to anybody in a disrespectful manner again. And if you're so anxious to get to school, sure I can get Tommy up the lane. I'm sure Tom wouldn't mind lending him for just the one day, and doing Mulligan a good turn. So there's not a bit of need for you to worry yourself."

I didn't know what to do or say. I did know that I had tried to be too smart and it had backfired on me. I scuffled my feet on the floor and then I looked up into the still angry face of my father. "I'm sorry Da for not calling Master Colgan by his proper name, but all the boys in the school always call him Colgan. And I'd love to go to the fair. I'll ask Mr. Colgan if it's all right with him first thing in the morning."

"Well now, my good man," said my father, "It's a powerful different tune you're singing now, isn't it? And if all the boys in the school took off their shoes and danced in a big fire, I suppose you'd think that you would have to do the same. I would expect any son of mine and your mother's to be fit and able to think for himself. But anyway we'll see. Maybe I'll just ask Tommy all the same. It would be too bad to keep you off school when you are so interested in all that's going on. Go out now and get the byre cleaned out, and make sure and give the roaney cow a quart of meal."

I went out with a heavy heart. Jobs that I normally enjoyed and took a pride in, perplexed me. I could not believe how silly I had been. I was convinced that my friend Tommy would be going in my place, and good friend though he was, that was just too much. I thought of the long, sunny, summer day in school, when I could have been out with the men at the fair. I planned words to say to my father, but no matter what words I thought of saying, I knew that they would only make things worse. He kept telling me that when a person is in a hole, which he does not want to be in, he should not keep digging, and now I knew I was in a hole. That seemed the longest evening of my entire life, and my mother singing old Scottish songs did nothing to brighten it, or lighten the load. In fact her good spirits and my father asking for another song, increased my gloom.

I went to bed and rolled about in unease. I opened the window, from which I had extracted Da's nails and managed to get the dog in, but even he failed to help. I could not sleep and I thought morning would never come. And then I dreaded its coming, for my father might order me to go to school on Friday as usual. I was in a cold sweat. Suddenly I heard my father's boots clumping along the corridor to my room. I managed to get the dog under the bed and ordered him to lie. I hoped he would not jump out when my father came in and give the game away.

The door opened and Da stood in the doorway, with one hand on the latch and the other on the door cheek. "So you're not sleeping," he said as though this was a very big surprise to him. "I was just saying to your mother that you'd likely be fast asleep hours ago, and likely dreaming of the great things that will be going on in the school. I just called up to see you and tell you to make sure and ask Mr.Colgan if he will agree to let you off for the day on Friday."

"Thanks Da," I yelled and almost jumped out of the bed in glee. My father turned and pulled the door almost shut, and I could see that there was a smile on his face, which threatened to break into a laugh. Then he opened the door a wee bit again and pointed to my bed, "And you'd better let that dog out to his bed," he said, still smiling. "If your mother finds out that he's in here, she's liable to kill the two of us." I was never great at the prayers, but I certainly said thanks that night.

James Mulligan lived about half a mile away. He had a big farm, over a hundred acres, which was huge at that time. He always described himself as a gentleman farmer, and both he and his father were known for being the awkwardest and worst tempered men in the country. They were usually fighting with some of the neighbours, and if no neighbour was accommodating enough to annoy them, they fought with each other.

One day I was helping my father to lap hay in Mulligan's field, when they suddenly fell out, and James rushed at Herbie with a pitchfork. The old man tried to escape by crawling through a hole in the hedge, into the next field. He got caught up on some barbed wire and this slowed his progress. All the same he had almost made it when James drove the pitchfork into his rear end with all his might. "You dirty, rotten, wee runt, ye," squealed Herbie, "That's damned sore, and my arse is liable to go septic." His final description of his son was colourful but unrepeatable.

"It'll not go septic, ye stupid useless auld cod ye," answered James trying to mimic Herbie's squealy voice. "How the hell would it go septic when you are bloody septic from the neck down since the day you were born?" And his list of expletives to his father, illustrated the marked development in bad language, which had taken place over a generation.

James and my father got on quite well. That was due, in most people's opinion, to the fact the James was terrified of my father. At that time Da was reckoned to be one of the strongest men in the countryside, and in his youth had been a noted fighter, fearing no one and besting most. He told James one day, that if James gave him any reason at all, he would carry the head off his shoulders, and bury the rest of him up side down in a flax hole. James must truly have believed every word because he treated my father with a respect that was a wonder to all the neighbours. This was the man whom I was hired to help. My father was scutching flax at Benburb, and the money was so good, that he could not afford to lose a day's work.

We reached the fair without any major incident. James sold his cattle as stores in the main square, and this was a new experience for me. I had to 'hoard', or keep the calves together while James bargained with the dealers or other farmers. If a calf attempted to escape, James addressed me in a frenzy of unbelievable language and threatened to eliminate me for my stupidity. I have no doubt that had my father been present James might well have ended up minus his head. But finally the calves were sold, James was delighted, and in spite of my protestations, he insisted that I come with him to the pub.

We took our places in the crowded, smoke filled bar, and James installed me in a corner. He ordered a whiskey and a stout for himself and various other drinks for a couple of neighbours, and then he told the barman to give me a 'red biddy.' "Do you think that is wise?" asked the barman, looking at me with obvious concern in his eyes. "He's only a cub, a child really, and that seems a bit strong at his age." He stood there with a puzzled and worried look on his face.

"Would you go and do what you are bloody well told," roared James. "Do you think I am stupid or what, and I don't know what I'm doing? Give the lad a red biddy and be quick about it. He's worked like a man all morning, not like an auld cissy like you, going about with an apron on you. I suppose you wear a lovely pair of nice silk knickers." And with that James threatened to take the man apart if I did not get a red biddy.

The talk and debate around the table took all the attention away from me. I looked at the slightly pink coloured liquid in front of me, and wondered how to get rid of it. There was a big plant growing in a pot in the corner and I was preparing to give the plant a big treat, when James turned to me suddenly. "Take up your drink there, lad," he said in a low but determined tone. " You've worked out there like a man all morning and you deserve to drink like a man." He lifted the glass to my lips and practically forced me to take a mouthful. It tasted not too bad, but caught the back of my throat and made me splutter. Again attention moved away from me and I started to sip at the glass but also managed to pour some into the pot beside me. Really once I got used to the taste, it seemed not much different from lemonade. I felt great and after a while laughed at everything anyone said around the table. The whole world seemed like one big joke. Normal events were hilarious.

I don't know how long might have passed when James turned to me again and said, "Come on lad, we can't stay here all evening. Joe Hughes is going home in the pony and trap, and he'll give us a lift to near Benburb." His voice was very slurred and I found it difficult to make out what he was saying. But I did realise that I was being offered a lift in a pony and trap, on a lovely summer afternoon, and that would have been like a dream at any time. Now it was like manna from heaven. I went to get up and rush out to the trap, and fell in a heap on the floor. My legs felt like rubber tubes and refused to do anything I wanted them to do. Otherwise I was quite sensible. I could not understand what had happened to me, but I knew that I must be slightly drunk. My father had told me about men losing control of their legs, when they had taken a drop of drink.

Mulligan gave a great guffaw of a laugh, got up to lift me, and went stumbling across the bar and ended up smashing his head into the corner near the door. Someone said that he was as drunk as a monkey, and in no fit state to take a child home. Blood was pouring from his head where he had hit it on the low latch of the door, and his shirt and jersey were slowly turning bright red. The general opinion was that he deserved all he had got and more. There was no sympathy for him but men were concerned about getting me home. Someone was sent outside to fetch Joe Hughes.

A few minutes later the messenger arrived back, and announced that Joe was sound asleep in the trap, and that if Mulligan, was as drunk as a monkey, Joe was as drunk as forty monkeys. By this time I had been helped to sit on a bench and all my functions were fine, except for my legs. There was a heated debate about what should be done to see that I got home safely. At last it was decided that if Mulligan was put in the trap, he would be capable of driving the pony home.

James, now covered in blood, was half led, and half carried out to the trap and installed on the left hand seat. Joe was snoring loudly on the floor and growling that it was time for Minnie, his wife, to get the cows milked and the hens fed. No sooner had he mumbled these words than James let out a fearful mouthful of curses and fell stone cold on top of him. No one knew whether he was asleep or unconscious. They did not seem to care. Their only concern was to get me home safely. "Be God," said one of the men, "If Mick Dawley hears about this handling, we'll be attending funerals for a week." Turning to me he asked, "Do you think lad, that you could manage to drive that pony as far as Hughes's, if we straightened you out on the road? By that time, one or the other, or maybe both of these eejets, will have sobered up?"

It was really my day after all. Never had anyone made a suggestion that thrilled and delighted me so much. To be allowed to drive the pony and trap on my own for three miles, was something that would be talked about

The Glow of the Oil Lamp

in the school for months and maybe years to come. I nearly fell out of the trap in my eagerness to get hold of the reins. And now my legs were starting to respond in normal fashion again. "I could drive that pony and trap to Timbucktoo," I assured the man. "No bother at all if you would start me on the right road."

The man took the pony by the head, and led him through the crowd until we were on the Armagh road, or as we called it then, the bog road. I knew I could make my way home from there, and I asked the man to let me have control. He did so but gave me a few hints on how to drive the pony. He stayed with me for quite a while and made me stop and start, turn right and left, back into a gate and do all manner of things that I knew I would never need to do. I enjoyed that lesson more that any lesson I ever had in my life. Finally the man waved me off, and told me that if I happened to find a hole deep enough, I should dump my two companions into it.

The journey was uneventful but truly delightful. I was in a state of pure bliss. I only wished that the pony would take smaller steps so that the joy would be prolonged. Most blissful of all, the school was on this road so that all the boys would witness me in my glory. We were about half a mile from Hughes's when Mulligan growled, asked where he was, straightened himself up, and inquired from me as to who the hell had hit him.

I explained to him that he had staggered into a corner in the bar, and had hit his head on the latch of a door, and that was how he had managed to get cut. He looked at me, the whites of his little brown eyes, red with anger. "Do you think I'm some sort of stupid eejit, that I'd believe a cock and bull story like that?" he squealed. I was really afraid for a moment that he was going to tear my head off. "Turn that pony round and we'll go back till I see the boyo that did this to me." I was very greatly tempted. It would mean that I would have to drive the pony for another four miles or so, and I could think of nothing I would rather do, especially as the boys would be getting out of school as we passed. But just then Joe Hughes woke up, crawled up onto the seat and seemed to be as sober as a judge. "Dammit lad, you are making a great job of driving that pony. Your Da will have to get you a pony and trap of your own. What the hell happened to Mulligan? Did some Fenian lockjaw him for being an Orangeman?"

I explained to Joe exactly what had happened while James protested that it was all a bundle of lies. "Close your bloody mouth, you brown skinned wee runt you or I'll lockjaw you myself," roared Joe. "And when you're at it, get to hell out of my trap before I kick you out." That in very diplomatic language is a summary of the conversation.

Mulligan and I started walking towards Benburb for that was now the nearest way home, at least it was for James. I was thinking of what Joe Hughes had said. I was marvelling in my mind how wonderful it would be to have a pony and trap. It would be heavenly to drive past the boys at school all the time in pride and dignity. But I knew it was impossible. We simply could not afford a pony. But imagination does not cost money.

The Glow of the Oil Lamp

And imagination and recollection kept me in enjoyment for many weeks afterwards.

We reached a corner where there is a sharp turn about half a mile from the village. There was a noise on the other side of a hedge, and looking in, we could see a man facing a hedge with a billhook. The man was a known character in the countryside and he claimed that he had been a leading member of John Dillinger's gang in America. It was explained to me that Dillinger had been on of the most daring and vicious of all the American gangsters, perhaps the most ruthless and dangerous man of his time. Apparently the rest of the gang were little better. Most people believed Bill's story and he had a flow of foul language and tales of horrible deeds to confirm their belief. Apart from my father I never met anyone who was not afraid of offending him. It was said that he would stick a knife in you as quick as look at you. Bill never did nor said anything to contradict this belief, for he maintained that you should never stick a knife into a man without giving it a good twist, when you had the blade in to its full depth. I knew a bit about his reputation, and was wary of him, for we passed the place where he lived, every day on our way to school.

I have not the slightest idea why he did it, but James went over to the hedge and started taunting old Bill with all sorts of insults. Bill made a bee line for a hole in the hedge, threatening to cut the heads off the two of us. I believed in my heart that he meant every word he said, and I think James did too. I am convinced that the only thing that saved us was that Bill got stuck on some barbed wire in trying to get through the hole in a hurry, and in obvious bad temper. This delayed him long enough to give us a fifty yard start. Mulligan ran up the hill as fast as he could, dragging me along with him by the hand. Bill chased us, waving the billhook in the air, and demanding that we wait to be executed. I have always thought that the language he used could only have been learned from the famous John Dillinger himself. I don't think I have ever been so totally frightened in my life, and I am certain that James was no better.

For the first hundred yards or so, Bill seemed to be gaining on us. But then, thankfully, we began to widen the gap and eventually Bill stopped, and throwing the billhook forlornly in our direction, continued to threaten torture and a slow painful death. Out of breath, we reached the village safely and finally got home in one piece. That night when my father came home from work, he asked me how things went, and I simply told him that we got the calves safely to the fair without any bother, and that as far as I knew they had made a good price.

A few days later, Dad and I were walking home from Benburb. We came to Mulligan's and James was examining a wall that he was having built at the end of his lane, or as he always called it, his avenue. The wall was nearly four feet in height and he was wondering what kind of top he should put on it. It seemed at first that my father was going to walk past without speaking. This was most unusual and it surprised me greatly.

"What kind of a top do you think I should put on this bit of a wall, Mick?" asked James, turning round to face us. "You have done a fair bit of building in your time and maybe you would have a good idea about it."

My father walked slowly over and stood about two feet away from his questioner. He made no attempt to answer the question but looked James straight in the eye. "You never told me what you did last week, you good for nothing deceiving rogue," was all he said. James leaned back against the wall with a hammer in one hand and pointed into my father's face with the other. "I only treated the lad right, Mick," he murmured, "I treated him better than you would yourself."

I cannot honestly say I saw Da move. But I was aware of movement, of tremendous power and a thump. The one thing that I do remember seeing, was the soles of James's shoes disappearing over the wall. "That'll maybe teach him to red biddy a child of mine," murmured my father, speaking it would appear, to no one in particular.

Strangely enough, James came to our house a few days later, to ask my father to help him with the cutting of the corn. No one mentioned that anything untoward had ever happened. All was forgotten between them. But I never forgot the red biddy and in moments of dreaming, I relive the joy of driving the pony.

CHAPTER 17
THE HOUSE AMONG THE TREES

It was the fifteenth of August and Tommy and I were lying at the top of Jordan's hill, our backs, supported by the outer rampart of the fort. I had just passed my tenth birthday and that morning after Mass, we had played around the yards and fields all morning. Now we were lazily looking out over our homes to the wooded country to the south, and enjoying each other's company. We were also enjoying the intense heat of the noonday sun and eager for something fresh to do. Already the countryside that I had known in earlier years was changing. No longer were we surrounded by the little whitewashed, thatched cottages, which had been replaced by asbestos roofed houses, finished in pebble dash. Our house remained as it had been, but all the others were rebuilt and extended, and for some of the neighbours an age of affluence had begun.

I noticed Tommy's eyes settle on the thick woods that lay in a deep valley slightly to our left, and far below us. I knew that he was dwelling on a very black patch in the centre of the trees, where a mysterious building called the old rectory stood. After staring at the spot for a few moments, he pulled a stalk of grass, bent it in two, put it in his mouth and began to chew on it slowly. Glancing sideways at me he asked in a carefully careless tone, "Would you have been in round the old rectory lately at all?"

My eyes darted instinctively to the dark shadow among the trees, and I felt a surge of fear mixed with excitement. I knew that Tommy was acting the 'big man' and I did not want to admit, that I had never dared go near the old house in my life. I was fairly sure that Tommy had never been there either, but of course I could not be absolutely certain. As coolly as possible I answered, " Naw. Not lately. Have you been round it yourself, or what put that into your head?"

Tommy sat upright and embraced his knees with his arms. The long piece of grass was now held between his teeth, its head and bottom resting lightly on his arms. He chewed nonchantly and answered, "There were a couple of ceilyiers in our house the other night. I heard Da telling them about it. They were saying that years ago it was a terrible bad sort of place."

I looked at him in puzzlement. "What do you mean years ago? Ma and Da say that it is a real death trap, and sure everybody in the country knows that it's haunted."

Tommy leaned further forward until his chin rested on his knees, and the stalk of grass hung loosely down in front of his legs. His eyes were fixed intently on the shadow in the trees. "Aigh. Right enough. It's haunted all right. That's what they were on about the other night. Micky Mallon was saying that his grandfather minded the time, when the ones that lived there owned all the land in the glebe. And he says that at that time they brought whole boat loads of girls over from France, and they were never seen again after they went inside the walls."

Now I was not only scared but puzzled too. I looked down at the dark spot where I knew the house stood in ruins. Mechanically I pulled a stalk of grass and started to chew it. Finally I asked, "And what in hell's blazes would they want whole boat loads of girls for?" It was a question that made me feel daft, but I could not help asking it. Tommy looked at me. His eyes had a far away empty look that told me that this was a problem which he had never considered. A vexed expression came over his face. At last he answered me a bit reluctantly. "I don't know what they'd want with them. Auld Mickey said that they used them, and then they got rid of them in some sort of pit that was dug near the cellars. Whatever they used them for it seems that they didn't last long at it."

I looked out over the countryside thoughtfully, and then down at the shadow of the old house. Then I spoke slowly as I thought my father would have done, "Be God, Tommy that would be a tarra. Wouldn't you wonder that nobody would have found out about it? Wouldn't you wonder that the police could not have got the wind of it?

They were quick enough to get down to our house about the dog a couple of months back, about whether he was licensed or not."

Tommy spat out on the grass and gazed reflectively out over the countryside. He answered in low tones that were almost inaudible, a technique that he had learned from his uncle Joe. "Mickey says that they put them in big barrels of acid, as far as the people were able to find out. He says that there's hundreds of people round the country who have heard them screaming and yelling in the middle of the night. He says that there was nobody who could tell what they were screaming about, on account of how they were shouting in French, you know. And Mickey was saying that he himself met a wee woman with a big black dog down the lane. He says he met her as often as he has fingers and toes. He swears that she walked past him and disappeared off the face of the earth. Oh that place is haunted all right."

At this point I rolled over on my side and looked up into Tommy's face. He was clearly aware of this but continued to sit and gaze into the heat haze that covered the county Armagh landscape, away to the south. He narrowed his eyes in thought, and pulled a fresh piece of grass to chew in the side of his mouth. I asked him, "What sort of light do you think that would have been, that Charlie Curran saw in the top windows of the place a couple of weeks back? Wouldn't you wonder what anybody would have been doing about the place at three o'clock in the morning?"

Tommy moved somewhat uncomfortably. He did not want to let me see that he had never been in or near the old house in his life and that really, like myself, he knew nothing about it. He glanced sideways down into my face. "Sure you wouldn't know what the hell it was," he said reflectively. "Da says Charlie got a big slap of drink and he fell in the sheugh, with the bicycle on top of him. Da says that he seen the moon from the bottom of the sheugh, and he thought it was somebody with a big light. But Mickey says that it was some craytur searching about for their soul. He says that there were so many people done in, about the place, that there's more ghosts around it than there's people in the town of Dungannon. And he says they wouldn't do you a pile of good if you went near them. But auld James that digs the graves says that the boys under the headstones never did him a bit of harm but he likes to keep a sharp eye on the boys that's walking about."

We both lay back and were silent. Without really being aware of it we both kept our eyes fastened on the dark shadow in the trees. After a while I got up on my elbows, and turning to Tommy I asked, "What'd you think Tommy if we took a walk down yonder and had a bit of a look around the place? There doesn't seem to be anybody about, and we could be back before dinner time. They'd never know anything about it."

The words were uttered in the bravest voice I could muster. Deep in my heart I was hoping that Tommy would find some reason as to why we should not go. But I should have known better for never in my life had I known Tommy to back away from a challenge of any type. In reality I think he had been toying with the idea of exploring the old ruin in spite of his parents' warnings. His quick answer chilled my soul, "Aigh. Come on. We have time enough. We'll dander down before they start looking for us."

The Glow of the Oil Lamp

Together we made our way down the steep hillside, and through the fields to the woods. Some of the fields were in grass so we were able to walk across the middle of them, but where we came to a crop of corn or potatoes we skirted along the edges, for we knew that we would be in serious trouble if we were found in the middle of a crop.

After ten minutes or so we came to the banks of a small stream, which we called the Yankee's drain. It was much cooler down here under the trees, that grew along the water's edge, and every few yards there was a swoosh of wings as pigeons rose from the trees, aroused from their midday siesta.

We stopped by every pool in the stream to watch the sprickleys dart about in the clear rushing water. The great fort of Sessiagh was now far away on top of the hill that dominated the countryside around. I felt a growing urge to suggest that we stop here by this peaceful stream and fish, but I did not want Tommy to sense my fear and trepidation. So we made our way slowly, beside the river, towards the object of my dread. We came to a small gateway where, on one side, the stonework had been knocked down to make the opening wider. At one time this gateway had led from the walled garden to the side lawn of the house, but now both sections had been joined to form an undivided grazing area.

We kept close together as we made our way into what had been the walled garden, and now the great menacing bulk of the huge square, three storey building, towered above us. It looked bleak and bare and cold, but the inside of my heart felt even colder. From some of the rectangular openings in the great grey walls, the dilapidated frames of ancient windows hung rotting, at all sorts of crazy angles. Others were simply black holes that had an eery look to them, probably because of the stories I had heard about the place. I remembered my father telling me that this house had once had a window for every day of the year, but one of them had to be built up, since it was against the law for any building to have as many windows as the royal palace in London. There was no walled up window in the side of the house at which we now stared.

There was a thick clump of bushes at the corner of the building to our left, and we rushed to hide there in case we should be discovered by the owner. A hundred pigeons and a huge flock of crows rose from the surrounding trees. For a time there was a flurry of wings and a cacophony of cawing, which seemed sufficient to alert every farmer in the countryside, but soon all was quiet again. We lay there, under the bushes on our tummies, our fear filled eyes absorbing every detail of the gaunt, lifeless mansion. Now only the sound of our bated breathing broke the stillness of this desolate place, as we rose to explore the rest of the site.

The front of the house looked exactly like the side from which we had come, except for the massive doorway with a set of wide steps leading up to it, and round marble columns supporting a heavy pediment above it. To each side of this, a deep pit had been dug along the entire length of the building in order to give light and air to the cellars. This pit had once been surrounded by wrought iron railings, but now it was guarded by a few strands of barbed wire, hanging from decaying wooden posts. Neither of us wanted the other to know that this scene was completely new to us. For some reason that I still do not understand, I said to Tommy, "I bet you boy, that you couldn't knock yon glass out of that window there, above the door," and I pointed to a lone pane hanging in a battered frame, which had once held eight similar squares of glass.

Tommy didn't answer but began to search for suitable stones. He was proud of his ability at throwing stones, and here was a challenge that he could not refuse. The first stone was hinched carefully but it passed through the empty section beside the glass pane. There was a moment of silence, and then it could be heard bouncing off a wall before it made its way down through the interior of the old house. There were many bumps and dull sounds as it plunged downwards, each sounding immensely hollow and resounding. We stood still, petrified, but in a few seconds all was quiet again. I grabbed a stone from Tommy's hand, measured the distance carefully, and threw with all my might, as though I had a special hatred at that lone pane of glass. But the stone bounced harmlessly off the masonry a couple of feet above the window, and dropped into the pit in front of the house.

It would be difficult to describe the look of contempt on Tommy's face, but this was rapidly replaced by a glare of sheer determination. Fixing his eye on the lone pane, he flung back his arm and with all the power in his body, sent a stone whizzing towards it. The stone struck the glass dead in the centre, and shattered it in a thousand pieces, before bouncing and falling and thumping through the darkness of the old house. The sudden noise of the breaking glass aroused the flock of crows from the huge chestnuts and beeches. They wheeled above the trees cawing angrily, and seemed to stay so forever before slowly settling back into the foliage. For a few moments it seemed as though we were in the blitz of the war, and we dived into the bushes once more.

We were ready to run for the river should anyone appear, but the minutes went past and once more all was peaceful. I turned to Tommy in sheer admiration, "Be God Boy that was some shot you made. You hit her dead in the middle. I thought for a while that the bloody crows were going to bring the whole country to see what was going on. Tommy, that stone seemed to fall a quare bit after it hit."

Tommy nodded slowly, clearly pleased with this praise of his ability. He was now gazing at the great door. He pointed to it. " Do you see that window just above the big door there, boy? If a body climbed up that wee wall that is at the side of the steps, you could reach that window and get inside. I would like to have a look round the auld place when we're here. I haven't had a chance to get a look at it this many's a long day."

A wave of gnawing fear swept over me. I felt as though every muscle in my body was frozen with some vague terror. The climb was possible, though dangerous, but I had never been a great climber. More than that, the thought of going into the old building after all the stories I had heard about it, sent a shiver through my veins. I stood looking at the old house but did not answer. "Well, are you going to stand there all day and tomorrow as well? You are like a cow chewing her cud." Tommy knew that he had the advantage and he was driving it home. I suspected that deep in his heart he was hoping that I would refuse to go.

I looked at him standing there under the bushes. There was a kind of smirk on his face and I knew that if I backed down now I would never live it down with him. I shrugged my shoulders and gave my whole body a shake as well, in the hope of removing some of the dread that was engulfing me. I squared my jaw as best I could and said, "Right. If it's the inside you want to see, I'll give you a hand. I wouldn't like to have to tell the boys at school that you'd never seen the inside of the old rectory. Sure every Sunday Michael Murphy and me are in and out of that place, like rabbits in and out of their holes. There's hardly a Sunday but we dodge in some time or other."

Michael Murphy was my cousin, some four years older than me, and he did spend most Sundays roaming the countryside around Sessiagh, but we had never been inside the old house. But if you tell a lie, sometimes you have to stand over it.

Stealthily Tommy and I made our way to the stone steps, glancing round every few seconds to make sure we were alone. We climbed the six steps, and stood by the side wall, looking up at the window just above our heads. The wall itself was shoulder high from where we stood, but on the other side, there was a sheer drop to the bottom of the pit. The floor of the pit was covered in slime, some twenty feet below, and through this, here and there, the spikes of the railing that had once protected it protruded menacingly. It reminded me of some animal traps that I had read about in books. A stale, damp, unpleasant smell wafted up towards us on waves of heat.

I climbed up on to the wall and perched on the shaky, crumbling coping stones that still clung to its top surface. Small pebbles were dislodged by my movements, and some of these fell on to the great flag stones at Tommy's feet. Others rattled their way into the pit and disappeared into the black mud there. "For God's sake would you watch what you're doing," growled Tommy. "You are rolling about like an auld clocking hen on a roost. If you don't watch what you're doing, you'll end up along with those stones in the bottom of that hole."

I glanced down into Tommy's face in annoyance, but said nothing. Instead I reached up and stretched my arms through the window opening above my head. I found I was just able to grip the inside edge of the window ledge, and I pulled myself slowly upwards until I was crouching in the opening. Slowly and awkwardly I turned round on the narrow sill until I was facing outwards. Glancing down I felt dizzy for it seemed a long way down to where a pointed spike stuck up threateningly out of the slimy dark mud that surrounded it. Slowly I manoeuvred my legs over the inside of the ledge and lay over it resting on my tummy. To my great surprise my feet found a solid stone platform only a small distance beneath the window. Once on solid footing, I reached down and gave Tommy a hand up, so that in a few seconds we found ourselves inside the great damp, cold building.

At first we could see almost nothing in the interior, until our eyes grew accustomed to the change from the brilliant summer sunshine outside. All was deathly silent and there was an unpleasant dampness in the air that one could smell. Gradually we were able to make out the lines of rafters, which hung precariously across the entire span of the building. Some had fallen away, some hung at crazy angles from the walls, and all were blackened and gnarled as though by fire. Here and there, odd bits of floorboards had survived on the two floors above our heads, and it was the same below in the deeper darkness that stretched through the other storeys to the floor of the cellars. The entire inside of the huge structure was a dark and dangerous skeleton, which seemed to glower at us from every corner.

The stone platform on which we stood was at the top of a flight of stone steps, which led down to the ground floor, near to the main doorway. It had once formed the first part of the flights of stairs that had connected the floors of the great house. But above this spot the stairs had been made of timber, and this had been stolen, or had rotted away in places, so that now only the shattered remnants clung desperately to the walls. Apart from the landing on which we stood, there was hardly a solid piece left in the place.

Tommy turned to me and said in a strained whisper, "God boy, the whole inside of the shanty is destroyed altogether. You'd think that the place had been burnt or something. I heard big Jim telling Da one night that Joe Crowe built all the sheds that he had about the place, with the timber that he got out of here. Do you see the way all the floors have been pulled up?"

I looked around in silence almost unable to speak, so overcome was I by the feeling of menace that pervaded the place. "I did hear Da and your uncle Barney talking about how some of the neighbours took all the timber and things out of it," I whispered. "Da said that there used to be a quare grand set of stairs, and that some of the quare grand people around the country decorated their houses with the grand timber."

"I wonder," said Tommy, "could a body make their way up to the roof. There's bound to be a quare good view of the country from there."

I looked upward. The huge old beams hung loosely in their sockets, and the sections of stairs, which remained, looked as though they were about to fall at any moment. The great square, heavy roof sagged downward at its centre and threatened to collapse into the cellars. The massive timbers of carved mahogany, which had supported the main structures, had been ripped away leaving the floor joists hanging in all sorts of positions. I knew that it was because the place was so clearly dangerous that Tommy wanted to climb to the roof. With terror in my heart and hardly able to get my mouth to form the words, I answered, "I suppose we could try it anyway."

It was not difficult to reach the first floor landing for here only a few bits of stairway were missing and we were already half way there anyway. But with every movement we made on the stairway, the whole structure groaned and creaked, and threatened to come away from the wall entirely. But when we reached it, the landing itself was solid, for it was supported by stone beams, set into the walls. There was an open window right above this landing, so here the place was well lighted.

But now we could see the difficulty of the task before us. The next set of steps was on the opposite side of the building. There was only one way of reaching them, and that was by crawling along one of the old floor joists that stretched right across the house. But these had been supported at the centre by the timbers that had been torn away. Now they relied simply on the fact that their outer ends were set fairly deeply into the walls. At the centre only light plaster held them together.

I edged myself out until I was straddle legged on one of the joists. Putting my hands a few inches in front of me, and swaying slowly forward on them, I began to ease myself carefully out along the plank. I had gone about four feet when the plank gave a great groan and moved sideways in the wall socket in which it rested. It lurched downwards in the middle at the same time, so that I dared hardly breathe when it became stationary again. I glanced fearfully around and saw that Tommy had begun a similar journey two joists away. "You're all right," he whispered reassuringly, "that stick that you're on would hold up a ship. Drive on your goat ye boy ye."

I was not so sure. The joist still felt as if it was wavering and it was definitely dipped at the centre. But

I did not want to be a laughing stock. Tommy was just about level with me when I reached carefully forward once more to begin my journey anew. My body was in mid movement to catch up with my hands, when the timber gave a loud crack in the middle and broke away entirely from the beam opposite. A shower of pieces of plaster went hurtling down through the building. The joist sat still for a second before starting to drop away at the centre, and slide out of the wall behind me altogether. I was terrified, paralysed. It was a nightmare.

The joist was already gathering speed on its journey to the cellars, when I flung myself sidewards with all my strength. I made a desperate bid to grab the plank between Tommy and myself. My arms were scratched by the rough timber as I flung them round it, but the joist was clutched to my chest. It felt solid and I did not think it would move. But the beam on which I had been sitting a second before was now plunging downwards to the cellar floor, bumping into other joists on its way, and taking some of them with it, together with a shower of stones from the hole in the wall, in which it had rested for generations. The entire wooden framework of the house trembled, and I think that for a time we both thought it was all going to collapse and take us with it. But eventually it settled and our joists remained in place. A swirling cloud of dust now filled every part of the building from the debris that had cascaded to the floor.

Tommy was still sitting on his joist, pale and shaken. He had not moved during the entire near fatal incident. I was still swinging in mid air, my chest and arms

The Glow of the Oil Lamp

feeling sore and tired. I tried to drag myself up onto the joist, but it was difficult for there was nothing to grip with my feet. A surge of panic swept over me and I could see myself plunging and falling and bumping downwards, just as the timber had done. A vision of my sorrowing parents looking at my mangled body flashed through my mind. I was desperate for I knew that in a few moments I would have to let go.

Tommy moved on his plank very slowly and carefully. He spoke in earnest but frightened tones. "Did you hurt yourself boy?"

"Not too bad," I replied, "but I can't get up on to this bloody plank. My arms and chest are as sore as hell for I had to jump hard onto this stick."

I was gasping now, my face red and swollen. "Try and raise yourself up and get your belly onto the stick," Tommy urged.

I made a great effort but had to give up. I nearly let go altogether and the big tears began to tumble down my face. I knew I could not hold on much longer.

Tommy wound his legs tightly round his plank and leaned over and grabbed my jersey and braces just at the back of my neck. It was a dangerous and tricky move but he began to lean back and pull as hard as he could. "Try and drag yourself up now," he hissed, his own face red with the effort. At this point there was a slight movement in Tommy's joist, and we both knew that we were near to death.

In sheer agony I began to ease myself up once more. Tears of pain and fear were tumbling down my cheeks. I managed to raise myself a few inches, and Tommy's weight held me. Another painful effort brought me to a position where I was swaying on the joist, with it digging into me just below my rib cage. Tommy still held me but even though the tears streamed down my face, I knew that now I could make it. "Swing your legs up and get them onto the plank," Tommy hissed through clenched teeth. "Watch out you don't tumble over and fall on the other side."

I swayed sidewards and with all the strength I had left, swung my legs upward to straddle the plank. But for the fact that Tommy still held me, I think I might have fallen with pain and tiredness. But I did manage to get astride the beam, and I lay face forward resting, Tommy's hand still holding my jersey. Glancing sidewards I saw that Tommy's eyes were streaming tears too, and he looked scared and shocked. I straightened up, but felt so sore and tired that I was still unsteady.

We were now facing each other for I had swung onto the beam in such a way, that I was now facing the wall from which we had started out. Tommy eased himself slightly backward, and as he did so his joist groaned and moved in its socket. He stopped, clearly petrified. I put both arms out and grabbed my beam. But the numbness suddenly left my arms, and I yelled in agony with the pain that replaced it. I had to take another rest before making the movement that brought me abreast of my friend. Tommy made another move backward, and again the beam lurched slightly under him. It was clear that it was getting more and more unsteady. Now I held his jersey lest his plank fall. It seemed like hours before we reached the stone platform from which we had set out. But together we scrambled onto it and lay against the cold wall crying. We were safe.

Together we scrambled down to the little window, through which we had entered. We helped each other to climb out and down to the front steps. I found it very hard to believe that we were once more out in the hot noonday sun, and breathing the clean healthy air. When we had started out from the fort some two hours earlier we were both clean and tidy, a credit to our parents on this important church holiday. Now as we stood together in the warm sunshine, I realised that we were both covered from head to foot in sticky black grime, and that my Sunday clothes were completely ruined. My mother had told me about how hard it had been to afford these clothes, and I wondered how I was going to face her. For a short moment I wondered if it would not be preferable to lie senseless at the bottom of the old house.

I suddenly realised that as well as covering them with dirt, I had caught my trousers on a nail somewhere, and that they were ripped from the waist to the knee and were hanging loosely around me. This really sent a pang of dread and foreboding through my heart, for I knew what a struggle it had been to buy them in the first place. It wasn't often that she beat me but she had a habit of reciting her woes in a plaintive voice that was much worse than any beating. I could hear her lecture on how hard it was to make ends meet - at one stage I thought she was saying 'hen's meat' - and I knew she had to deny herself to run the home. Tommy and I looked at each other with dread in our eyes.

The Glow of the Oil Lamp

"Be God, Arthur," said Tommy, "we're in a quare fix now. You look like a nigger that fell down a chimney and into a threshing machine."

"You're not that powerful clean looking yourself," I growled back. "Look at the whole front of your trousers and your jersey. Your mother will kill you stone dead for do you mind when we were leaving, she said not to get a spot on you."

Tommy looked all over his clothes, and then tried to clean them with a handful of grass. The dirt, however, was damp and sticky and only spread further. He looked at me out of the side of his eye.

"Look at the way your trousers are hanging round you," he said with a titter of laughter. "As sure as God you look like an auld woman with a straw arse. Be God, here, I say, your mother will be good crack to listen to, when she gets a look at you. I heard her bragging in our house the other day, about the terrible price she paid for them trousers. My mother said after she went out, that you'd think that nobody ever bought a pair of trousers in their life before. Be God, boy, I wouldn't like to be you when she gets a hault to you. You'd be better off if you went down a hole and lived with a badger."

I felt a deep pang of despair. I knew that all Tommy had said was true, and that he was getting a certain amount of satisfaction out of it. I took a long look at him and tried to think of something equally destructive to say. But while he was pretty messed up I knew that I was much worse. As well, my arms and chest were now stinging sore and with one thing and another, I felt close to tears. We made our way along the river bank in silence.

We reached Tommy's house at last, and decided to slip in and try to get cleaned up. But to our utter consternation we walked straight into Tommy's mother, coming out of the barn. She had been feeding a wee calf that had no mother. A thin woman of medium height, Julia had a bucket in one hand and milk was still dripping from the other. She wore a bag apron over her Sunday clothes, and she stared at the two of us standing before her. She stood in stunned silence for a few moments, and when she spoke it was with obvious anger and annoyance.

"Oh God, Oh God, where in heaven have the two of ye been? Look at the cut of you. Look at the state of your good clothes. Under God what's going to be done with the pair of you anyway?"

As she spoke the anger was rising, and she dropped the bucket to grab Tommy by the left ear. "Where did you get yourselves in this state of dirt?"

With each word she gave the captured ear a strong upward tug, and it was clear that each tug hurt. I shuffled about in embarrassment and discomfort. I did not answer nor did I think it was my place, and I could not think of anything to say anyhow. But I felt guilty and ashamed for Tommy was suffering for something that I felt I had started.

"Oh Ma, Oh Ma, mind my ear, go easy will you." Tommy was hopping about on tiptoe, and trying to take the pressure off his ear. His mother, however, still held him tightly, and by now the redness was showing in his face even though it was covered with greasy slime.

"Oh Ma, Oh Ma, would you look at your clothes?" Tommy's mother was mimicking him and twitching his ear with every phrase. "Oh Ma, just take a look at your clothes and take a look at the bold Arthur. When his mother sees him she'll skin him alive as sure as there's an eye in a goat. That is, if she doesn't kill him stone dead first."

This prediction did nothing to lessen Tommy's discomfort, and it petrified me, for I had been doing my best not to think of meeting my mother. I knew that I was a worse case than Tommy, and I considered my mother an impossible person to deal with when I was in the wrong. Even my father would seem to wilt at times before her swingeing tongue. I started to pray for some sort of miracle even if it meant the earth opening up to provide an escape route.

"Ma, we fell into the sheugh down at the lough Ma. We just slipped off the bank."

Tommy squealed the words, standing on the very tips of his toes. His mother chose this moment to release him, but made a swipe at him that he had to dive smartly sideways to avoid.

"And what were you doing down at the lough? Don't you both know that you were told, over and over again, never to go next or near it? Didn't I hear your Da telling you the other day to stay away from about it? How did you fall in and get all that dirt?"

" We were crossing the stick down at the boat track, and Joe Bogan took a hold of the stick an turned it and we fell off into the mud. Do you see the way he tore Arthur's trousers? He did that with a big sharp stick when we were trying to get out."

At this point Tommy skipped over beside me, and extended the torn garment for his mother's inspection. I had been standing gaping open mouthed, as the story of our misfortune unfolded. It was a moment before I realised that Tommy was now exposing my person to the world in general, and to his mother in particular. Feeling myself go red and getting flustered, I grabbed the bedraggled trousers and clasped them around me. Tommy's plan had worked, and his mother's attention was now fully on me. She came over and examined my heavily soiled clothes. I was so embarrassed that I squirmed and twisted away from her. She now spoke to me in kindly, considerate tones for she was like a second mother to me.

"Oh God save us all son, you can't go home like that. That young Bogan fellow should be drummed out of the country for leaving any mother's child in a state like that. If I see any of them around here again, I'll take the hide off them. Come on into the house here, son, till we see what we can do to get you fixed up."

We walked sheepishly together into the newly renovated house behind Tommy's mother. We entered the kitchen with its dresser, and its line of cream crocks on a stool along the back wall and the big table of scrubbed whitewood, over by the window. By the wall opposite the fireplace stood Julia's two most prized possessions, a tall polished mahogany gramophone, and a treadle driven Singer sewing machine. These things had been her mother's before her. She immediately went to the sewing machine, and removed the cover. Then she turned to me. "Give us them trousers there, lad, till I see what we can do with them. Your mother'll knock the very head clean off your body, if she sees them the way they are."

If Tommy's father had not now been blocking the door I would have taken to my heels. As it was I was bent over double, caressing my pants and hopping about in embarrassment. I could feel my cheeks burning red, and the tears starting to drip down them as well. Mrs Jordan saw my plight and she understood. Immediately she turned to Tom, her husband.

"Tom," she said, "would you take this lad up the house, and get him some sort of a pair of trousers or something to cover him up? I'll try to do something with the ones he's wearing before his mother gets her eyes on them."

Tom now spoke for the first time, but he had been standing with his shoulder against the wall, almost since we had entered the house. "Under God, Julia, what were you and them two cubs up to anyway? What were you doing that they got their bits of clothes into a shape like that?"

Tommy did not trust his mother to handle this situation adequately, so he butted in. "Arthur and me were coming home, down by the lough, Da, and we were crossing that big stick down at the boat track. Joe Bogan was there before us Da, and when he got the two of us on the stick, he got hold of a pole and twisted it and tipped the two of us into the mud. And Da, he tore the whole trousers off Arthur, as Arthur was trying to climb up the bank out of the mud. Do you see the state of Arthur's clothes Da?"

Tom was still leaning against the wall, his right hand resting on a horse's collar that was sitting on the window sill. His eyes turned full on his son and he asked, "And what did you do on Joe Bogan before he did the likes of that to you?"

Everyone looked up at the big man. He had spoken slowly, through the right side of his mouth for he held his pipe in his teeth on the left side. He began to slice tobacco with a penknife, using his right hand now to cut the slices carefully into his left palm. His eyes and all his attention appeared to be given to this task, for he did not look at us at all. He simply continued to pare away at the black plug while sucking the empty pipe with an air of absolute contentment. We knew this picture and this attitude well. We felt that Tom was talking to us man to man as he did to the neighbours on their ceili. Tommy gazed up into his father's face, and his eyes were big and earnest.

"We did nothing on him at all Da. One morning in school, before the holidays, Colgan had us all lined up to get our exercise marked, and Joe threw Arthur's book up onto the flat glass window that was open. Then he shouted to Master Colgan to take a look at what Dawley had done with his book. Before anyone had a chance to say anything, Colgan grabbed Arthur, and beat the arse off him, and stood him under the clock. And there was Bogan up in his seat laughing the ears off himself."

The Glow of the Oil Lamp

"And did you let Bogan away as light as that?" There was just the right element of surprise in Tom's voice.

"No, Da. That evening there was a big fight down at the bridge and Arthur beat the tar out of him. But Bogan got his own back on us there a while ago."

Tom was now rubbing the tobacco in the palm of his left hand, using the heel of his right hand to do so. He was a self-confessed expert at the job and obviously took a great deal of intense satisfaction from it. His eyes slowly lifted to his son and he reached up and tipped back the brim of his hat with the extended thumb of his left hand. There was a puzzled expression on his face, which was belied by the twinkling amusement in his eyes. When he spoke he addressed not only Tommy, but everyone in the room, and it appeared also, some omniscient, invisible being.

"I wonder now," he said in slow reflective tones, "who would that cub have been who gave me a hand a while ago, to cap three wee calves that broke out of the end field? That would have been the big part of an hour ago, and sign nor sight of you two boys could I find about the place?"

There was silence now but for a slight scuffling as we shuffled our feet in unease. Julia, who had been standing silently beside the sewing machine looked hard at her husband. She spun round to catch Tommy a resounding clip on the ear, that made him cry out in astonishment. "Oh, Ma, Ma, would you watch my lug? What did you hit me that clout for?" His mother did not answer but spun round in the opposite direction and caught him an even better clip on the other ear.

The Glow of the Oil Lamp

"That'll even the two of them up for you." She hissed bitterly glaring into his eyes and in obvious bad temper. "You come home here with your clothes a parcel of rags, and then you have the cheek to tell me and your Da a bundle of lies."

"What lies Ma?"

Tommy had asked the question before he had given himself time to think. He was carefully watching his mother lest she deliver another smack on his ear, when his father reached forward and caught him. In one swift movement with his left hand he lifted the boy and drew him across his knee, while with the other hand he unbuckled his thick leather belt. He had administered four solid strokes before Tommy quite realised what had happened. He was back on his feet again before the seering, stinging pain began to spread across his bottom and throughout his body.

I stood wide-eyed in fear and embarrassment, and half expected Tom to grab me next. But the big man stood lighting the well filled pipe, which until now, he had never taken from his mouth. His eyes quietly gazed through the curling clouds of smoke. Those eyes never left Tommy's face, and I knew that I was an outsider here. There was silence for a time in the room except for the sucked in hisses that Tommy made in response to the stinging spasms in his aching bottom. It was in this interval that we heard the sound of approaching footsteps on the gravelled lane outside. No one said a word for we all knew the light foot of my mother. My heart seemed to miss a beat. I felt a surge of sudden sickness in my stomach, and there was a lightness in my head so that I thought I was going to faint.

At this juncture Tom turned quickly, took two steps and stood with his right shoulder leaning on the outside door cheek, holding the other cheek with his left hand. He was effectively blocking passage into the house. Smoking peacefully, he gazed up at the great fort in front of the house, almost as if he had never seen it before. He appeared to be totally unaware of anyone else in the vicinity. "Ach hello Sarah. How are you doing at all? Isn't that a fine sort of a day?"

Tom's voice had a faint air of surprise in it, which indicated that my mother was the last person that he expected to see. "Hello, Tom, it's a fine day all right." There was no mistaking my mother's strong Scottish accent. She was proud of the fact that her accent had never changed. "Would you have seen the two lads at all Tom? I've the dinner ready this last hour and a half, but I can't see Arthur about the house or around the land."

I looked down at the floor for I was aware that the eyes of Tommy and his mother had swung onto me, and that they were sizing me up. I pulled my shattered clothing more tightly around me, and at this point I felt a pang of envy for Tommy because I reckoned, that at least he had the worst of the bother past him. It seemed a very long time indeed before Tom's quiet, reassuring tones answered my mother's question. "Aigh, Sarah. Sure they're all right. You needn't worry yourself about them at all. They're doing a wee job for me just at the minute, and as soon as they're finished I'll send the lad

The Glow of the Oil Lamp

home. You know how they like to get finishing a job that they like doing."

There was a very long moment of awkward silence while my mother failed to respond. It was not she minded in the least that Tom should ask us to do a job. She knew he was a kindly and caring man with a great way with youngsters. But it was the first time since she had come to Sessiagh that she had arrived on the street without being invited into the house. Now, however, he stood blocking the doorway and it was clear that this was one time when she was not going to be allowed to enter.

"It's all right Tom," she finally said with a bit of an edge to her voice, "I'll maybe call and see you when you've a bit more time to spare."

We knew by the sounds that she had turned on her heel, and set off smartly for home. Tom had to smile to himself at her parting remark, for it would have been hard to imagine anyone with more time to spare than a man contentedly smoking and viewing the countryside. But his smile was rueful too, for he knew that my mother was exceptionally sensitive, and he feared that there would be coldness between them for a while. At last he turned and came back into the room. It was to me he spoke. "Well now, my fine boy, do you see the bother that you have got me into with your mother? Come on down the room here till we see can we get you some sort of thing to put on, till Julia sees what she can do with the trousers."

I quietly, ashamedly and sheepishly followed him into the bedroom. Tom went to a cupboard first, and then not finding anything suitable there, he opened a wardrobe. Without looking round at me he threw a shirt of his over his shoulder and said, "Pull that jersey and those trousers off you and put that shirt over yourself till we see if Julia can do anything about all that mud and that rip. Where the hell did the two of you get into that shape anyway?"

I did not answer and he now selected a jacket from the wardrobe and turned to face me. I was still pretending not to have heard his question while I reached under the shirt, which I had put so as to cover me while I removed my trousers. I felt in my heart though, that Tom knew his son's story was untrue, and at one stage I was on the point of blurting out the whole truth of the incident. But then I thought that such an action would be a betrayal of my friend, so I kept quiet. I pretended to be so busy getting my clothing fixed that I had no time to answer.

Tom stood in the middle of the room with an amused grin on his face, gently pulling at his pipe and watching me all the time. When we had made our way back to the kitchen Julia began work on my trousers, and Tom turned his full attention on the two of us as we sat beside the embers of the small summer fire. I was holding the 'men's clothes' as tightly as I could around me, and feeling decidedly uncomfortable.

"Wouldn't it be quare craic," said Tom in a reflective sort of voice, "If I had warmed young Bogan's lugs for him the next time I met him. Do you know I might just have been a big enough eejet to do that, if he hadn't been giving me a hand with the wee calves when he was supposed to be couping you boys into the lough?"

Tommy looked at me and I looked at Tommy, but neither of us said a word, and we both pretended to have developed a sustained interest in the patterns of the fire. "Now, my good men," said Tom, directly and sharply, "where exactly were the two of you this last two hours and more?"

Tommy gave a deep sigh, and seemed to grow smaller on his stool. Then he slowly straightened himself up as though it was a great effort to be forced to tell the truth. He looked at me sadly first, and then slowly his gaze rose to his father's stern face. Another big sigh indicated the depth of sorrow that was in his soul for having led his parents astray.

"Oh Da," he sobbed, " I'm real sorry for telling you and Ma a pack of lies. I don't know what put it into my head to do it at all. We got into the muck on account of how we were helping Mrs Allen."

I gave a sudden and audible gasp of surprise, and I looked suddenly up from my toes, which I had been studying assiduously. I hoped that my astonishment was not as obvious to others as I thought it must be. But the rationale behind Tommy's new story was clear to me. The Allens lived on the other side of the fort, and that was not the direction in which the rectory lay. Tom was lighting his pipe again. He glanced down sideways from under the brim of his hat and asked, speaking through clouds of smoke, " And what might the two of you have been doing at Allens, that you got yourselves into that sort of shape?"

Now Tommy was relaxed again for the soft enquiring tone of his father's voice gave him confidence. He now looked confidentially up into his father's face, peering through the smoke that swirled around them. "Well, you see, it was this way Da. Allen's big game rooster got out of his pen, and Mrs Allen was afraid that he would kill all the fowl about the place. She had been running after him and you know how she has a gammy leg at the minute, where she fell off a chair when she was painting a ceiling. With the bad leg there wasn't a chance in hell of her catching him. Arthur said to me that it would only be fair to help the poor woman out. Was that wrong Da?"

Tom gave a sudden start at the unexpectedly direct and apparently innocent question. He seemed about to move towards his son but then settled back into his former posture. Slowly he pushed back the brim of his hat with his outstretched thumb and answered Tommy quietly in a very understanding, fatherly manner, "Not at all Tommy, there would be nothing at all wrong with the likes of that. I would expect any son of mine to help any of the neighbours who needed help, and I know Mick Dawley would do the same. It was real good of Arthur to think of that. But then Arthur's the very best of a lad, so he is."

I squirmed in embarrassment at this unjustified praise, but Tommy's face lit up with renewed confidence. "Well, Da, Arthur and Mrs Allen chased the rooster round the yard, and he flew up onto one the pig houses down at the back yonder. Arthur followed him up over the pig house and on to the roof of the turf shed.

He was up on the ridging of the turf shed and he was just about to fly off, when the boyo here made a dive, and got hold of him by the foot. But Arthur slipped and the rooster and him tumbled down the slanty tin, and on to the big dunghill at the back of the yard. Arthur's trousers got torn on a big nail that was sticking up on the edge of the pig house roof, but he never let go of the rooster. Do you see the way the boyo cut the whole inside of Arthur's hands with his big spurs?"

Tommy grabbed my hands and held them up to his father for inspection. It occurred to me that the cuts and scratches made by the planks, could indeed have been made by a rooster's spurs. But at the same time I felt rather foolish as Tom's gaze rose from studying the hands to looking into my eyes. I felt as though I were being led deeper and deeper into a maze, and I did not see anything that I could do about it. But now Tommy continued his explanation.

"Mrs Allen says Da, that Arthur's as good a lad as you'd find anywhere in the whole of Ireland. And you know Da, I heard you saying one day that it's not often Mrs Allen praises anybody, only her own."

I could see evident laughter in Tom's eyes as he now looked at his son. Pushing back his hat to scratch the top of his head, he asked, "And if Arthur got his clothes destroyed doing a good turn for Mrs Allen, what happened that you got yourself all dirty and nearly as bad as him? As far as I can make out, from your story, you were happy just to stand there, and watch the neighbours doing their duty?"

The Glow of the Oil Lamp

Tommy reacted instantly. He looked at his father with an air of injured disgust. "Da," he said, " Nobody said that Arthur got dirty on the roof. He only tore his trousers there. It was after that, when we were giving Mrs Allen a hand with the big sow and the new litter of wee pigs, that the old sow knocked the two of us down and that is how we got our clothes destroyed."

Tom did not answer but he leaned over close to his son and sniffed at the surrounding air. "Wouldn't you think that after rolling about through all that pig dung, you two boys would stink the house out?"

Julia turned from her work at the machine, put her nose in the air and she too sniffed, "Right enough, Tom," she said, "There's no trace of the smell of pigs at all. There's a damp dirty smell right enough, but it's definitely not the smell of pigs."

Tommy looked at me, as though for inspiration, but finding none, he looked down at his soiled garments and then into the embers of the fire. A moment later he looked up into his father's face, "But Da," he gasped, "That old devil of a sow knocked us down in the yard yonder. There's only muck and old cow dung and no pig dung. Isn't that right Arthur?"

He gave me a solid kick on the shin in case I might have fallen asleep. I shuffled uneasily. I looked into the fire hoping to find some clue as to what I should say or do. But I did not want to get drawn into this intimate family discussion. I had some sort of vague idea that my friend was being led into dangerous territory, and I found it hard to think of anything to say. At last, feeling that I had to say something, I nodded and whispered,

"That's right. There's nothing but cow dung in Allen's yard."

Tom threw back his head and gave a howl of laughter. He stopped, rubbed his eyes and then threw back his head and gave another howl. I was completely lost as to what was amusing him. At this point Julia got up from the machine and went over to the fire to place the stone of her smoothing iron at the heart of the flames. Next she got a basin of water and some soap and she began to sponge my jersey and trousers, trying to remove the grime. After a few moments, during which everyone watched her in silence, she looked up at us. "Oh God, Oh God, Tom," she cried, "I don't know what sort of dirt this is at all. It's all grease and you'd think it had been made in the cloth. And I don't know if the iron is going to take it out or not. Tommy run up the house and bring me down that big sheet of brown paper from under the bed."

Tommy departed energetically on his mission, and his father leaned forward to knock out his pipe against the hob in front of him. Mrs Jordan was sponging away for all she was worth. I sat huddled on my stool hoping that nobody would ask me a question while Tommy was out of the room. I could think of a thousand questions, which would land me in the soup, but I could not think of one evasive answer. But Tommy arrived back, carrying a big sheet of brown paper before anyone spoke.

Julia laid one section of the paper carefully on the end of the table, placed the trousers on top of it, and then folded the other part of the paper on top of them.

Taking the long tongs she went over and removed the stone from the fire and slipped it into its box. When the stone had heated the iron to her liking, which she tested by running her free hand over it, she set to work ironing on top of the paper. As the strong heat penetrated, wet grease stains spread across the paper. It looked as though the job would be a success. Tommy stood watching his mother as did his father, and I could not take my eyes off the spreading stains on the paper. After a few minutes Tom asked in a slow puzzled voice, "Tommy, I don't know who those two cubs might have been that I saw coming along the Yankee's drain a couple of hours ago? It was just at the time young Bogan was giving me a hand with the cattle. They were so dirty and bedraggled looking, that you would have taken them for a couple of tramps."

Tommy looked as though he had been hit in the face with a brick swinging on the end of a rope. He looked his father straight in the face because he did not know where else to look. Tom looked straight back at him with an air of enquiry on his weather beaten face. At that moment Julia took a hand in the proceedings once more. Leaving down the iron she grabbed Tommy by the ear so that the boy had to leap up and dance on tip toe around her to ease the pressure on the ear. "Oh God Ma, my ear, my ear. Hi there, go easy on my ear or you'll pull it out by the root. Hi, hi, go easy, go easy on my poor lug."

The boy's pleading had no effect on his angry mother, except to make her actually increase the upward pull and painful pressure on the ear. She now used her free hand to wallop him on the bottom. Her eyes were pools of rage and she was red in the face. "You wee brat you," she yelled at him. "You useless wee brat. I don't know what kind of a rearing you are, under God on this holy day. It's not enough that you ruin all your bits of clothes and give me all this bother, without you having to tell your Da and me a pack of lies, that would choke the very devil himself." This speech was accompanied by many attempts to get good thumps at his bottom and Tommy was now looking very sorry for himself. I felt totally out of place in this family quarrel, but here I was, right in the middle of it, and feeling that I deserved at least as much punishment as Tommy. But I was an outsider with no place here.

After about a minute or so of his mother's offensive, Tommy at last burst into tears and began to bawl like an infant. This had the desired effect for he was released and was able to caress his aching ear. At this point Tom sat down on the stool by the fire and with his elbows resting on his knees began to fill his pipe again. At the same time he sat gazing into the fire in a state of total tranquillity. It was as though he had been marooned on an island of peace. But suddenly he jumped up, and looking all round the room, shouted, "Good God, Julia, there's something burning. Is the house on fire or what? What did you do with that iron?"

Everyone's gaze now swung to the table, where a steady column of smoke was now rising from the brown paper on top of the trousers. It had taken us a long time to detect the smoke for it was being wafted out through the open window by the breeze coming through the front door. Julia rushed over and pulled the iron away but it had already burned its way through the paper and the cloth. The trousers were now ruined beyond repair and the poor woman stared at them in horror, holding her hands on top of her head. The large section where the iron had been, was a mass of crumbly soot. Leaving the iron on its stand she turned to her husband. " Jesus, Mary and Joseph, Tom, what are we going to do now? That lad is going to be the end of me." And running across she grabbed Tommy by the ear again. "That's you and your lies and carry on," she yelled and was about to slap him again when Tom took hold of her.

"Hold your horses there, Julia," he said gently. "The lad told lies and he did wrong; the two of them did wrong, but he has had enough for one day. You can't blame him for ruining the trousers, it was our fault too."

Julia went back to the table and stood again with her two hands on top of her head, staring at the ruined material. "Oh God in heaven, how am I ever going to face your mother, Arthur?" she asked, without looking at me or turning round. "Maybe you and me would be better to clear out of the country altogether. She'll go stark, staring, raving mad." Julia's consternation did nothing to soothe my nerves nor lessen my dread. I had already been dreading trying to explain to my mother how I had ruined the trousers, but now I began to wonder if I should ever venture home at all, and I thought, perhaps, there was merit in Julia's suggestion.

Tom was now sitting astride the stool, the dead pipe clenched in his teeth. He was clearly studying the expressions on my face and that of Julia. Then he pushed back his hat with his thumb, threw his head back and gave a great roar of laughter. Everyone stared at him as though he had gone suddenly mad, but our looks only made him laugh the more. With tears of laughter running down his cheeks he spoke to Julia through his mirth, "By God, my good woman, but isn't this a quare handling that you've got yourself into now? And poor Arthur here along with you. I'd far rather face a badger with a litter of pups, down a hole, than Sarah Dawley when she sees what the two of you have done to the good trousers. Be God, she'll take the very hide off the two of you." Here he threw back his head to laugh once more.

Julia took two steps, which brought her right in front of him. It was clear she did not see any joke and her face was grim and threatening. She looked directly into her husband's eyes and held a pointing finger just under his nose, "Well now, my bold man, so you'd rather face a badger down a hole would you? Well, maybe that's just what you're going to have to do. You sat up there smoking and minding other people's business, and the whole house might have been on fire. So now for your bother you can have the pleasure of taking Arthur and his trousers home. I wouldn't like to deprive you of facing the badger in her hole if you're so fond of it." At this point she grabbed the ruined trousers from the table and plopped them in his lap, showering him with soot in the process.

" And what would it be that would make Tom have to face the badger in her hole?"

Everyone in the room turned sharply at the question posed in the well known Scottish accent. We had all been so interested in the trousers that none of us had heard my mother approaching. She now wore her soft house shoes, so that she did not make any sound. She stood, hands on hips, just inside the door, surveying the scene. Julia made a despairing effort to hide the trousers on Tom's lap. I curled up on my stool and prayed earnestly for some of the gifts possessed by the invisible man. But my mother's eyes were glued to the garment on Tom's knee.

"Under God, Julia, what happened to the child's trousers?" Then turning sharply to me without waiting for an answer she demanded angrily, "How did you do this to your good clothes?"

I looked despairingly at Tommy and then at his father, seeking some help or inspiration. Tom got up slowly and stood facing my mother. Gently he put his big hand on the little shoulder, and when he spoke it was in a kind of whisper, "Did you know we have had a hell of a morning here, Sarah? The lads went down to the old rectory, and they got themselves all covered in muck. Julia here was …."

He was cut short at this point by an unearthly scream from my mother. Suddenly she rushed over and pulled me into her arms, and I could feel her body trembling against me. An instant later she grabbed Tommy and pulled him into her arms too. In this fashion she held the two of us for a long time panting as though out of breath. Finally she let us go, and stepping back, looking at us, said, "Let me see you children. Are you both alright?"

She turned to look up into Tom's puzzled face, and her own face was covered in tears, which were now tumbling freely down her cheeks. " That's what I came up the lane to tell you Tom," she gasped. "Bill McKenna called at the house and he told me that the whole roof of the old rectory has collapsed and the whole house is down."

For a long time there was silence in the room, but for the sound of peoples' breathing. The three adults were gazing at each other in horror, seemingly unable to move. At last Tom said, "Tommy, take Arthur up the house and see if you can find him a pair of trousers so that he can go home for his dinner."

"I ruined his trousers….," began Julia.

"To hell with the trousers," interposed my mother, "as long as they're alive! The Mother of God must have been looking after them this day."

The three adults sat huddled round the fire giving thanks for their extraordinary good fortune. Down in the room Tommy fitted me out with a pair of his trousers, and I was just about to leave when he grabbed me by the shoulder. Looking fiercely into my eyes he hissed, "Do you see the way Da knew all the time what we'd been up to from the start? There's one thing you can be dead sure of Arthur, you can never trust your bloody parents."

The mansion house in Benburb, built by James Bruce, who bought forty nine townlands and the people in them, in 1886. For the past fifty five years it has been a Priory run by the Servite fathers.

CHAPTER 18
INVOLVEMENT IN A BATTLE

The year nineteen forty six was a memorable one, for anybody living in our part of the country. It was in that year that celebrations for the three hundredth anniversary of the famous Battle of Benburb, were held. It so happened that at the beginning of the year, Fr. Peter Moore, our local curate, bought Benburb castle and its grounds, for the parish of Clonfeacle, our parish. The purchase annoyed the parish priest at first, because he thought that his curate had burdened the parish with a debt, which they would never be able to pay. One day my mother walked to the Moy to do some shopping, and the parish priest gave her a lift in his car on the way home. I remember her coming into the house and telling my father, "Poor Fr.Soraghan is nearly astray in the head with worry. He says Fr. Moore has no sense and has landed him in a hole that he might not be able to get out of."

The castle had been built by James Bruce, the last landlord, when he bought the Benburb estate in 1886. The estate encompassed forty nine townlands, and totalled nine thousand, two hundred, and sixty acres.

The Glow of the Oil Lamp

The Powerscourts, who were given the original lease in 1603, were in deep financial difficulties by the 1860s, and they put the property up for sale. It had no 'big house' as the Powerscourts had been absentee landlords, who lived in Wicklow and Dublin, and had no need of a house in Benburb.

Bruce, who was a rich whiskey distiller, bought the entire estate, and then set about changing it to suit his aspirations and desires.

As soon as he became the owner, Bruce decided to build himself a castle, or manor house, which would reflect the fact that he was now an extensive landlord, and the equal, he hoped, of the landed gentry. He cleared one side of the old village to make a site for his new house, on a level area at the top of the steep banks, which rise up from the river Blackwater, to the village. He moved the tenants, who lived on that side of the street, to other parts of the estate, and their descendants still live there at the present time. Bruce continued to live in Belfast, and only used the huge house at Benburb, for a few weeks each summer. It is said that his wife detested country life, and was not overly fond of country people.

The new house, of sandstone and brick, was built on a marvellous site, looking out to where the city of Armagh lies in the distance to the south east, and the hills of south Armagh can be seen on the horizon. It dominated the gorge where the Blackwater had cut its way through the limestone cliffs, and where the Ulster Canal had been brought up through the gorge, by means of seven locks, which are said to be an example of engineering, unsurpassed anywhere. In the early part of the twentieth century, however, the landlords were forced to sell their estates by law, and when Bruce died childless, in 1917, all that was left of his estate, was about three hundred acres around the village.

The manor house and its grounds changed hands a number of times, prior to the Second World War, but nobody could make a success of it, and by the outbreak of the war, all that was left was some sixty acres. During the war, the house was taken over by the British authorities, and was occupied by different groups of soldiers, British, Belgian and American. The Americans were the last, and to us children, the most exciting, for they gave us chocolate, sweets and oranges. They gave us rides too, in their great tanks and jeeps, so that there was competition to be their friends.

One day I was coming home from school, and had just passed through the village, when a jeep with two soldiers in it, pulled up beside me. They invited me to get in, and when I was in, they showed me a map, and asked me if I could tell them how to get to a spot marked with an X. I was no expert at map reading, but I realised that the marked spot was our house. When I told them this they sped off, following my directions, and when we reached home, we found a big tin can nailed to a post at the corner of the barn. In this can there was a notebook and some sheets of paper, which the soldiers filled in and put back in the can.

They seemed very pleased with themselves, and talked and shook hands and laughed, as though they had won a great victory. Then one of them turned to

The Glow of the Oil Lamp

me, and asked if I would do him a very big favour. He wanted me to take down the can from the post and nail it to another post, which was round a corner and could not be seen by anyone standing on our street. He explained to me that some of his friends would be following, and he wanted to play a trick on them, but he dare not move the can himself. If I moved it, he would not be responsible, and if I did so, he would reward me with a box full of candy. The bargain was made and I went to move the can.

My mother saw me with the hammer, and she wanted to know what I was up to. She had been working in the bottom room, and had not heard the jeep arrive. Now she came out to see what the soldiers were doing. When I went to take down the can from the post, she stopped me, and turning to the soldiers, asked if we would get into serious bother, and if the can was government property. Would the whole family end up in jail? The soldiers assured her that no harm would come to anyone, the whole thing was a game, and he simply wanted to play a trick on his comrades. But they also wanted to be able to swear that they had not moved the can. One of them then searched in the jeep and handed my mother a parcel, which she opened to find half a stone of sugar and a bottle of whiskey. Before she could say a word they started off, but noting that I was moving the can, they threw me a box of candy.

In less than half an hour, another jeep with three soldiers arrived on the street. They searched up and down, studied maps and had arguments while I watched them, happily eating away at the candy, and seated on the window sill. At last they called me over and explained that according to their maps, there was supposed to be a can on that particular damned post, and they asked if I had seen another party of soldiers. My knowing smile, and the fact that I had most of a bar of chocolate in my hand, must have made it clear to them what had happened. I ended up making a bargain with this group for two dozen oranges, in return for which, I showed them the can and promised to nail it to another post, which was even more difficult to find. That evening nine or ten jeeps arrived at intervals, and the result was that I ended up with more chocolate than most shops, and about two crates of oranges as well. In the following fortnight at school, I made a small fortune and my father had lots of oranges to share with his workmates at the mill.

The anniversary of the battle fell on 5 June, and since Fr. Moore and the parish now owned the site where the Irish leader, Eoghain Ruá O'Neill, had encamped on the evening prior to the battle, there was to be a double celebration. In school, Mr. Colgan began to teach us something of the history of the battle, and explained to us how O'Neill had totally defeated the army of a Scotsman called Monroe. I remember him berating me, and telling me that I should be ashamed of myself, for not knowing about a famous battle, which had taken place within a few miles of my home. I wondered at the time, since he had never mentioned it to us, how he expected me to know anything about it. It turned out that my father knew a little about it, though he had never mentioned it either. He, like Mr. Colgan, was scathing about the fact that I should be so ignorant, but he was able to help me with the essays, which I had to write about it during that spring.

Mr. Colgan explained that O'Neill had been training an Irish army for some time in the County Cavan. He was getting money and arms from the Pope in Rome, and was able to pay his soldiers very well. He knew that the English had three armies in the north, and in June he learned that they intended to join together at Glaslough, in the County Monaghan, and then move south to face him in battle. To stop this happening, he rushed north, and on Thursday, the fourth of June, he camped on the banks of the river at Benburb. His aim was to stop the main army under Robert Monroe, before it could join up with the others. On that same evening Monroe had encamped at Hamilton's Bawn, which is about four miles on the farther side of Armagh city.

Monroe set out from Hamilton's Bawn at four o'clock on Friday morning. He arrived in Armagh at eight, and was on the Blackwater, opposite Benburb, by eleven. He found the river crossing impossible, because O'Neill's forces held the steep banks and were well armed. Monroe decided to go upstream and find a ford where he could cross. At two o'clock in the afternoon, he was able to cross the river at Caledon. His army had marched twenty miles the previous day, and now on the Friday, they had already covered another twenty. They must have been very tired.

They took a short rest at Caledon, and then started to march towards Benburb. All this time O'Neill's army had been resting, and watching everything that was going on, under the shimmering summer sun. Monroe was convinced that O'Neill would never face him in battle, but would retreat to Charlemont fort, some five miles downstream. In the afternoon O'Neill sent some of his best cavalry units, to intercept George Monroe, who was coming from Coleraine to meet Robert. They surprised George Monroe's forces near Dungannon, and after a short fight George's men were wiped out.

While this had been happening, Robert Monroe was moving slowly towards Benburb.

At seven o'clock in the evening, his army crested a steep ridge, to find O'Neill's army drawn up in battle formation on Drumflugh hill, which is about a mile from the village of Benburb. While the two armies faced each other, they heard the sound of horses in the west. At first Monroe thought it was George coming to his aid, but the cavalry joined O'Neill. It was the moment Eoghain Ruá had been waiting for, and he gave the order to attack. The ensuing battle only lasted about an hour, and the English army was totally defeated. It is said that Monroe lost over three thousand men and O'Neill only about seventy.

Mr. Colgan explained that it was a great story. He told us that it was difficult to understand why Monroe did exactly what O'Neill wanted him to do. He allowed his men to become exhausted and he did not see the danger. Mr. Colgan said that the only reason he could see for this was over confidence. And he warned us that over confidence was something we should guard against for the rest of our lives.

The preparations for the big day were enormous, and entailed hundreds of people, not only from our parish, but from many surrounding parishes as well, working long hours to get the place ready. The house and grounds had been neglected over many years, and day after day, gangs of men with all sorts of tools, laboured to recover paths and other features, which had once been James Bruce's pride, but which had been lost to the undergrowth in the intervening years. Women were given the task of preparing food for hundreds of important guests, who had been invited from all over Ireland. By the beginning of June everything that could be done, had been done, and everyone was looking forward to the big day.

News leaked out that, for the big day, the organizers had found a red haired youth in County Cavan, who was called Eoghain Ruá O'Neill. There was a lot of publicity in the papers, about how this young man would be the guest of honour at Benburb because of his name and his red hair. At that time, John O'Neill, who lived across the fields from us in Sessiagh, had a young son, also called Eoghain Ruá, and who had a mop of red hair into the bargain. O'Neill's next door neighbour was Joe Allen, and he got pretty perturbed at the idea of these fools going away to Cavan to find an Eoghain Ruá, when there was one beside them in the townland of Sessiagh. Joe was a Protestant, but unlike most of his co-religionists, he took a great deal of interest in everything that was going on in Benburb.

My father did a lot of work for Joe from time to time, and that summer Joe had talked him into digging a well in the yard at the back of his house. I am not sure why Joe wanted this well, because he had one at the front of the house, and I used to help him in the evenings to lower creamery cans of milk into it, so that the milk would keep fresh until morning; it acted as a natural fridge. At the beginning of June my father was already down seventy feet, and he used to come home at night, exhausted and irritable for it was heavy, tiring and frustrating work. It was a job, which very few men would tackle, because it took great skill to keep the walls perpendicular, and it took great nerve to work in a confined space at that depth. It was Joe Allen himself who took the waste soil from my father, using a long rope and a bucket. Three long ladders, roped together, were required to reach the bottom. They had to be lifted above my father's head or out of the well while he was digging, in order to give him room to work.

One day, just before noon, my father could not understand why Joe was taking so long to come and get the next bucketful. He started to shout but there was no reply, and he began to wonder if Joe had had an accident. It must have been very frightening, trapped there at the bottom of the well, as the ladders were just out of reach above his head. Finally he sat down, sweating and uncomfortable in the confined space. It was frightening too, because he knew that water was liable to break through at any moment, and he might be drowned, for if the spring were strong, it would fill the well very quickly and there was no escape. Unbelievably he sat there for nearly four hours, until

Joe, all apologetic, came back to lower the ladders and release him.

Joe had met young Eoghain Ruá O'Neill and was overcome by a fit of pique and anger, at the stupidity of the people who were in charge at Benburb. He put the horse in the cart, and taking the youngster with him, he set off for Benburb in order to show the child to the people of the village, and especially to any of the people who were running the celebrations. He completely forgot about the well, and about the man sweating and swearing at the bottom of it.

When my father got out, no explanations nor expressions of regret would soothe his temper. He grabbed Joe, who was a big, strong man himself, and he shook him over the well, holding him by the braces and not heeding his pleas for mercy. John O'Neill came on the scene, and eventually managed to pacify my father, and persuade him to release Joe. John reckoned that it was very lucky that Joe had good braces, for that was all that saved him from a drop of seventy feet. In winter evenings of the years that followed, I often heard my father relate the story, especially on nights when John was one of the visitors. John took a special delight in getting my father to describe his feeling while trapped seventy feet down a well.

A few days after this incident, my father was persuaded to finish the job, as no one else would attempt it. He struck water at eighty four feet, and it rushed in so quickly that, had Joe not managed to lower the ladders instantly, he might well have been drowned. I discussed the sinking of Allen's well with Dad years later, and he assured me that being trapped in a well for four hours, does tend to shorten one's temper. I reminded him that, in my opinion, it had never been very long in the first place.

THE BATTLE AT BENBURB

On the fifth day of June ere the chill summer dawn
I was roused from my sleep near to Hamilton's bawn.
By his tent in our camp, in the dim pre-dawn glow
I could see our commander, Major General Munroe.

On his fine battle charger he filled us with joy
As he swore that ere noon, O'Neill he'd destroy.
Like him, t'was a contest we could treat with disdain
'Gainst a rabble of peasants, and some idiot from Spain.

Monroe looked like a God in his armour so fine
And my heart filled with pride as I stepped into line.
We reached Armagh city and the sun was now bright
Full of faith in our leader we were keen for the fight.

When we left the old city it was eight of the clock,
And we marched to the westward, to Benburb's great rock.
T'was a three hour hard slog over ground that was rough,
And many were thinking that we'd marched far enough.

For the hot noonday sun was now high over head
And our lightest equipment seemed heavy as lead.
And here 'cross our pathway the deep river runs
On its steep western bank, O'Neill's men and his guns.

There was no hope of progress; Monroe seemed at a loss,

The Glow of the Oil Lamp

My sore feet were wishing that he'd lend me his horse.
But the general faced his army and he said, "We'll go west,
We'll find a good ford and we'll there take a rest.

As we made our way upstream I found it no fun
That the foeman was basking in the hot summer sun
We plodded ten miles and at last found a ford,
As we marched into Caledon, I breathed 'praise to the Lord.'

For I was feeling sick and tired, my feet blistered and sore
My whole body was screaming that it couldn't take much more.
But we were soon on the march again, downstream to the east
While on each distant hilltop, O'Neill's men held a feast.

I was tired and weary but we kept marching on,
It was fourteen long hours since we'd left the Bawn.
In the evening we forded the Oona's slow course
On a hill to the north O'Neill watched from his horse.

Then at Thistle Hill Monroe gave us great heart
Saying, "O'Neill has to run away, there's no doubt of that,
For he let us cross the Oona, he scarce fired a round
And George has just joined us as you can hear from the sound.

And then were heard the hoofbeats of horses in the west
We raised a cheer of triumph, knowing our cavalry's the best.
But that died with us sadly as the horsemen joined the foe,
The finest of our cavalry had been slaughtered by Eoghain Ruá.

The Glow of the Oil Lamp

Downhearted we trod onward and then on Drumflugh's brow,
We saw O'Neill's whole army in massed formation now.
We fired off our cannon, but they firmly held their stand,
And then they charged upon us and met us hand to hand.

They were fresh and we were tired; the long sharp pikes were strong,
I knew that Monroe's planning has gone completely wrong.
We opened lines of passage to let our horsemen through.
But the long strong pikes held steady and they were beaten too.

And they fell back amongst us, there was no place to go
We were trapped there at the river by that genius Eoghain Ruá.
In one fierce hour of slaughter I was wounded in the head
And I fled across the river o'er the bodies of our dead.

In the fear filled days that followed I lay hidden in a bog
Expecting to be hunted and to face death like a dog.
But pursuit did not happen and we regrouped our force
And in spite of Benburb's battle we held on in the north.

CHAPTER 19
THE VALUE OF A TEN SHILLING NOTE

It would be fair to say that very few families in our area, were directly affected by the death toll or suffering, of the Second World War. Fred Roleston, the local grocer, however, had a son who was taken prisoner when shot down over Germany, was found to be badly injured, and eventually died. Our neighbour, James McMullan had a brother, who was a prisoner of the Japanese in Burma, was reputedly tortured and starved, and although he survived imprisonment, was a broken man when he got home. Most of the people whom I knew well were Catholic, and, therefore, less likely to have relations deeply involved.

On the other hand my mother's family living in Glasgow, spent night after night in the air raid shelters, and her brother, he of the sacred cycle, was an electrician, and had to work most nights during the blitz, in order to keep the power functioning. I have no doubt it was important and dangerous work. According to the stories my mother told me, he was the most gifted worker they had, and I think she was of the opinion that without him, the city would have been in permanent darkness.

Mother's sister, Bella, had married a Frenchman called Paul deSachet, some time in the twenties. They had a son called Maurice who was born around 1927. Very shortly after the birth of his son, Paul took diabetes, which was very serious at that time, since the use of insulin was a very new discovery, and he died a short time later. Bella lived only six months more, and my mother told me many times, how she had died of the same disease. Since diabetes is neither infectious nor contagious, this seems at best questionable. It may have been a coincidence but equally, she may well have died of some totally different cause. Tuberculosis was rife at the time, but people felt that it was a great shame to have this disease in the family, and would go to great lengths to hide the fact that one of their relations had died from it. At any rate, the orphan was accepted into my mother's family and for a couple of years before she came to Ireland, my mother had a lot to do with his rearing, and was extremely fond of him. She talked about him very often and I have vivid recollections of feeling that I had a cousin in Glasgow, who was a serious rival for her affections. Indeed it would be no exaggeration to say, that I felt I was very much in his shadow.

Much to the consternation of the family Maurice, joined the air force when he was only seventeen, apparently having given false information in order to be accepted. My mother was very worried when she heard of this development but she received a photograph of him in uniform, of which she was very proud. Concerned for his safety she talked of him incessantly, prayed for him daily, and recruited everyone she could think of, to pray on his behalf.

My father got up one morning at half past four, for he had to be at work at half past five. He left my mother sleeping, and was taking a cup of tea by the fire, when mother gave a screech, and came running down to the kitchen. "Oh, Jesus, Mary and Joseph, Mick," she screamed, "I am after having a dream, and I saw a plane crashing, and I know poor wee Maurice is dead. Oh Jesus, Mary and Joseph, what am I going to do at all?" My father tried to placate her, and persuade her that dreams could not be relied upon, but she was inconsolable. She went to the calendar and marked out the date with a blue pencil. It was 6 April.

Communications were very difficult in those days. Her family did not have a phone, and letters took a very long time to arrive, and were censored where families of servicemen were involved. I remember letters arriving with the words all blocked out, and nothing left but black lines. About all one could read were the address, the greeting, and the signature at the bottom. There was no news about Maurice, and my father did his best every day to persuade mother that no news was good news. She cried a lot, and spent long periods gazing at the blue cross on the calendar. I remember feeling blocked out of her life, and I did not know what to do about it. She seemed to be in another world. There was a great sadness over the whole house.

Six weeks went past, and one morning a normal letter arrived from her sisters in Glasgow. It informed her that Maurice had been taking part in a training exercise at Lossiemouth, early on the morning of 6 April, and the entire crew had been killed. The information had to be deduced, because my aunts took it for granted that mother already knew, since some of the earlier mail had contained detailed information on all that had happened. It was quite a while before the full story was clear to us. The plane had taken off, something had gone wrong at two hundred feet, and it fell to earth like a stone. For years afterwards the calendar remained hanging on our wall with the blue cross marking 6 April. My father was dumbfounded, and my mother took a long time to get over the tragedy. I cannot explain how or why these things had happened; I only know that they did. The story of the blue cross became a topic of conversation for miles around.

At this time my father joined with Jack McGuigan of Benburb, and the two of them took land on which to grow flax or corn. Da had grown flax on our land a year or so before, but flax is a crop, which takes an awful lot out of the ground, so that it was not wise to grow it in the one place year after year. In fact most farmers preferred not to grow it on their own land at all if they could help it. It was a crop too, which demanded very hard and unpleasant work. The preparation of the ground and the sowing were much the same as for any other crop, but when it came to harvest time, however, the flax had to be pulled by hand. This was a job for a boon of men. They were neighbours, all of whom had flax, and they joined together and moved from field to field, and from one man's crop to the next.

There used to be friendly rivalry amongst the women of the neighbourhood, as to who could give the men the best food. The same rivalry was rampant at threshing time too, when a big crowd of men had to be fed as well. My mother loved to have steak for the dinner, and prided herself that no one could outdo her in the preparation and serving of a meal. Julia Jordan had different ideas, and the rivalry between them was intense. Sometimes the women had to tie the flax into beets using bands of rushes, which had been prepared beforehand, but my father would never allow my mother to attempt this heavy work. Beets were exactly like sheaves, but for some reason got a different name.

Nearly every farm around us had a flaxhole, and some had two. The flaxhole was usually part of a sheugh, which had been widened to thirteen or fourteen feet, and it had to take water to a depth of three feet or slightly more. The flaxhole was filled with water and left for a few days while the flax was being pulled. This made the water soft and tepid, for fresh water would harm the crop. A trench was dug to divert any rainwater away, so that it could not mix with the water in the hole. The flax was put in with the heads of the beets to the bottom, and stones or sods were put on top of the flax to keep it down in the water.

After about ten days the flax had to be taken out of the hole. The beets were now much heavier and had a truly revolting smell. It was said that if you went to a dance after being in a flaxhole, you wouldn't be the most welcome of guests. I remember Jack McGuigan coming to our house at three o'clock one morning, to get my father out of bed, to take a crop of flax out of the hole in our field. One man had to get into the hole and hand the beats out to the other man, who would build them on the bank. Stark naked was the only reasonable way this work could be done. The middle of the night was, therefore, a judicious time to get the job done, when no one was about.

The next part of the operation was to spread the wretted flax, in order to let it dry. The bands on the beets were loosened and the flax spread over the field or fields, and left to dry. Often women would do the spreading, while the men were pulling somewhere else. This process depended on the weather, and when it was dry, it had to be lifted and formed into beets again. It was then built into stooks. For some reason these stooks were different from the four sheaf stooks that were used for corn. There were twelve or fourteen beets on the bottom part of a flax stook, and then seven or eight were built on top, so that it was a two storeyed construction. The stook had to be thatched with grass, cut from round the edges of the field with a scythe. Sometimes it was put into shigs, and sometimes it was taken straight to the mill from the stooks. It was a long, laborious process, but fairly lucrative in the years of the war, and for some time afterwards.

One year my father and Jack took a six acre field from Alex Skelton of Benburb. It was along the road between our house and the village, and they grew a great crop of corn in it. The corn was being harvested and my cousin

The Glow of the Oil Lamp

Michael Murphy joined us one day. While the men were working, we were trying to find something interesting to do to pass the time. Michael found a piece of the tree trunk, and he laid it along the bank of the sheugh, which ran along the top of the field. On it he began to place any objects that came to hand, such as jam pots, big stones, and sticks. He explained that these were targets, and he bet me that, standing about twelve feet away, I could not knock down six of them with ten stones.

I quickly gathered a pile of reasonably sized stones, and proceeded to show him that I was not as bad a shot as he seemed to think. I did not particularly notice that as soon as I was ready to attack the targets, Michael withdrew to a distance of fifty yards or so, to watch my efforts. I had only thrown four or five stones when I was attacked by a swarm of angry wasps. The targets had been set up in such a way that stones thrown at them, were bound to land in the wasps' nest. I fled to where Jack and Da were busy stooking corn, and they used the sheaves to beat off the attacking wasps. I was very lucky in that I only got three or four stings, while Michael thought it was the funniest thing he had ever seen.

Nearly sixty years later, Michael, who now lives in England, was on a visit to our house. A friend of mine is an ardent beekeeper, and I had given him permission to place a few hives in an old garden. I was showing Michael around the place, when he was suddenly attacked by some bees, which were apparently very annoyed by his presence. He got a couple of stings, and he swore that I walked him into the bees on purpose. It was a totally unforeseen situation, but at the same time

I reckoned it was nothing less than just retribution, for what he had done to a child.

My father got quite friendly with the American soldiers when they were in Benburb and on one occasion they brought him into the manor house for a drink. One drink led to another, and in the end Da got very drunk. It was a very wet night and Barney Jordan found him lying in a stream at the side of Sessiagh brae next morning. Barney said that Da's body was blocking the stream, and turning the water out onto the road.

Barney managed to get him out, and said he got nothing only abuse for his efforts. The result was that Da took a very bad cold, which turned into pneumonia, and he was confined to bed for nearly a month. It was the only time in his life when I remember him being ill, even though he took no care of himself.

My mother was very worried and as was her wont, she talked over all her worries with me. At first she was worried about his state of health, but as he began to show signs of recovery, she became more concerned about money. The only money coming into the house was from the hens, and it was not sufficient to keep things going. It was late October and there would not be much money available until the turkeys would be ready in December, and until that time they had to be fed. The rent was due at that time too, and she was scared that we would lose the place. The rent, as people called it was paid to the Land Commission, and went to pay off the price of the farm. It was a kind of long term hire purchase agreement, which allowed people to buy the freehold of their farm. People, however still

The Glow of the Oil Lamp

remembered the days of the landlords when families could be evicted if the rent was even one day late. My mother was in a state of dread, but she used all the money she had to pay the rent, and hoped for help from somewhere.

I took a bad cold or flu at the same time. Da was up in bed in his room, and now I was in bed down in mine. My bad cold only lasted a couple of days, and as I was getting better my mother came with a cup of tea, and sat down to talk to me.

"Oh Son, I'm nearly astray in the head," she moaned, "this is only Saturday, and I will not get any money until the eggman comes next Wednesday. Your Da is still weak, and he might not be back to work for weeks. Oh Son, I don't know what we're going to do at all. I paid the rent this week, and I'm glad that's done, but I needed the money to keep the house going. Oh God, my head's astray."

I looked at her sitting there with the tears in her eyes. It felt like the end of the world as I knew it. I sat up in bed and asked her, "What sort of money do you need to last till the eggman comes, Ma?"

"I have no money left at all Son. I spent my last sixpence on bread today. It could take six or seven shillings to get us through until I get the money for the eggs, and there's no where that I can get it." The big tears were now tumbling down her cheeks.

I reached over to the table at the side of my bed and lifted my copy of 'Red Cloud', a book that Mr. Colgan had given me to read. I opened the book and took out a ten shilling note, which I had saved from the money that my father paid me each week. I handed it to Mother and said, "There's a ten shilling note Ma. It's not much, but it's all I have, and I've saved it in the last few months from the money Da gives me. Would that be any help Ma?"

It was clear that Mother could hardly believe her eyes. She looked up at the ceiling and put her hands over her eyes and said, "Oh, Dear Jesus, am I seeing things? Has the child really got ten shillings or is it my imagination? Lord, I know I am so worried, that I could see anything."

She took her hands down slowly. She looked for a long time at the note I was offering her. Then she looked up into my eyes and I could see gratitude, relief and happiness in her eyes, which were now pouring big tears of joy. It would not matter how much money I might manage to get in the rest of my life, it could never match the depth of emotion I experienced that day. I had learned the potential value of a simple ten shilling note, and I still remember that lesson with deep gratitude.

I will go up to the altar of God and I will do my best to behave myself, which will be something of a change.

CHAPTER 20
INTROIBO AD ALTARE DEI
(I'LL GO UP TO THE ALTAR OF GOD)

Not long after I had changed schools, someone, I think it must have been Mr. Colgan the headmaster, decided that I should be an altar boy. The news greatly delighted my mother, who immediately set about fitting me out for the job. She bought a length of black cloth in Armagh of the highest quality available. It did not matter what it cost, her son must appear in public, dressed to perfection for the altar. She took me to the local dressmaker and between them they measured me for the soutane. It was decided that the soutane should have a large turn-up round the bottom, and corresponding ones round the cuffs. I think they believed that once I became an altar boy, I would grow to be a lot bigger than Goliath. The soutane had a row of very small buttons down the front so that when I put it on, I looked like a mini priest.

At the same time she had purchased a piece of fine white linen, and a length of four inch beautiful lace. Out of this they made a surplice, which covered the top half of my body, over the soutane. Other altar boys used

The Glow of the Oil Lamp

the surplices and soutanes, which were available in the vestry, but mother was convinced that these were not up to the standard necessary for me, and she was completely delighted with the results of her efforts. She instructed me to bring the garments home every week so that she could see if they needed to be washed, and if the surplice needed to be ironed and starched. If I were to be the only altar boy ever to come out of Sessiagh, she wanted me to be a credit to the townland.

My father was pleased too that I was following in his footsteps, because he had been an altar boy himself in the parish of Eglish, a generation before. He still remembered the Latin responses, and he was a great help when, each night, Mr. Colgan gave me one or two of these long Latin sentences to learn off by heart at home. They were to be found at the back of the old Maynooth catechism, and altar boys had to know them off by heart in order to respond to the priest at Mass. One thing puzzled me then, and it still does to this day. No one bothered to translate the Latin for me, though it is likely that Mr. Colgan could have done so. I remember asking one of the older boys who was on the altar, what it meant, and he told me to go and get my head boiled, for nobody bothered as long as we were able to bawl it out in answer to the priest. The priests were adamant that we should enunciate the words clearly, but they never explained the meaning of what we were saying. Very few in the church had the slightest notion of what it meant either. The whole procedure was a complete mystery to me.

I started serving nine o'clock Mass in Clonfeacle chapel, and I was to continue to do so for some three years or more. I do not think I was ever late, and I never missed, thanks to my parents. The three mile journey was no great problem for I had saved up my work money, and bought a small bicycle from my cousin, Michael Murphy. My father fitted a carrier to the back of it, and I could carry my stuff easily and safely. I used the bicycle for a good number of years until I left primary school. Everything was fine except for punctures. I became quite convinced that if there was a thorn in the country, which was not growing on a bush, it would find its way into the tube of my bicycle. The result was that I found myself giving the biggest part of my weekly half crown to Dick Wilson, who was our local bicycle repair man.

Dick lived in a tin house about a quarter of a mile outside the village of Benburb. His house had been erected, some years earlier, by a man called Tom McMullan, who had come home from New Zealand or Australia, and decided to build a house in the style of those countries. He probably wanted to show the locals how things should be done. The outer shell of the house and the roof were all corrugated iron, and it still stands there to this day, though both Tom and Dick are long gone. I seemed to call with Dick almost every day. It usually cost three pence to have a puncture mended, and Dick enquired if I had a special supply of thorns somewhere, which I drove into the tyres in order to keep him in work. Later my father taught me how to mend punctures, but even he came to the conclusion that my bicycle had been specially made to stand on its saddle and handlebars. But, these minor irritants apart, the bicycle was a great boon.

By this time bicycles had become very common even though the roads had not improved much. The main roads were tarred and in reasonable repair, but minor roads were still gravelled and could be full of potholes and pretty rough. Riding a bicycle often meant waving about in order to avoid these blemishes, but since there were hardly any cars it was not particularly dangerous. While I was one of a very few boys who took a bicycle to school, going to chapel was a totally different matter. Most men and women in the parish came to chapel on a bicycle, so that there was a collection of bikes parked along the graveyard wall, for each Mass. There must have been well over a hundred machines of all shapes, makes and sizes and they were parked four or five deep in places. At that time one could leave a bicycle anywhere and be sure that it would be there when one returned.

An altar boy was expected to be an example of good behaviour to the parish. But sometimes the carry on that took place on the altar would not have been tolerated in the body of the church, nor indeed, in any place where reverent people were gathered.

One Sunday a new boy was serving Mass for the first time. He was standing at the left hand side of the altar, waiting for the priest to finish reading from the book, so that he could carry it round to the other side on its heavy wooden stand. I was kneeling on the bottom step just behind him. While he was standing respectfully with his hands joined in front of him, I reached under his soutane, undid his shoe laces, and then tied them together so that there was a ten inch piece of lace, fixing one foot to the other.

He lifted the book to begin his journey round the altar. He stopped and glanced down at his feet, but since he could not see them beneath his soutane, he must have thought that his foot was caught in the flap of his trousers, or in the bottom of the soutane. Taking very small steps, he made his way slowly to the edge of the altar, but when he tried to step down to the second of the three steps, he lost his balance entirely. As soon as he began to fall, his arms shot out in a reflex action, and the book and its stand went flying across the altar railing, and into the front seats of the church. A large lady, who was saying her prayers with bowed head, got a great surprise when the heavy book landed on her chest. Her companion, a tall thin lady, who was her sister in law, got an even greater shock, when the wooden stand almost decapitated her. The incident was greatly to the amusement of many in the congregation. One could hear giggles of laughter for some minutes afterwards.

I rushed over to help my fallen comrade, who was stretched out on the floor, just inside the altar rails. A quick pull untied the lace, which had been held on a running noose. Everyone was busy attending to the two ladies in the front seat, and I hoped that my actions would be seen as concern for my colleague, and that no one would notice the undoing of the lace. Within a few moments it was decided that the boy had simply not tied his laces that morning, and that they had tripped him up. He was unhurt, which was lucky since he had fallen down three fairly big steps. The Mass finished and I went home, happy that I had been ingenious in covering up the trick I had played.

Next day at school, Mr. Colgan asked me to stay in at lunchtime as the parish priest was coming over, and wanted to see me. Fr. Soraghan, was a small, kindly man, who had been a great athlete in his younger days, and he was a great favourite with the children of the parish. But as soon as he came into the room it was clear that he was in a foul mood. He took me down to a corner of the room, and with Mr. Colgan beside him, asked me what I thought I was doing on the altar the previous day. "I was serving Mass, Father, like I do every Sunday." I knew I was in deep trouble and I could not think of anything sensible to say, and I knew my answer sounded cheeky.

Fr. Soraghan took me by the chin and forced me to look up into his eyes. "Now, my smart young fellow, we'll have none of your insolent answers. I asked you what you were up to yesterday morning on the altar of God."

"Well, Father, I was serving Mass, and when Francie tripped and fell, I went and tried to help him." My chin was still being held and I found it difficult enough to speak. I could see the frustration and anger in the priest's eyes, and I knew my evasive tactics were all wrong. It appeared to me that he knew exactly what answers he wanted, and did not need to ask the questions.

"Look," he said sternly, "It's a great honour to be allowed to serve on the altar. Even the greatest of the angels would love to come down from heaven and change places with you. The very least we can expect is that you are on your best behaviour at all times. Now what were you up to yesterday?"

"Well, Father, there were a few funny things happened, and I got a fit of the giggles. I could not stop laughing. We all found it hard."

"Oh, so you found it hard did you? And did any of the other boys think of tying Francie's laces together so that he could not walk, with the holy book in his hands?"

I was being forced to stare into his eyes, and I could see the anger rising there all the time. I could not think of a thing to say. I knew it was useless to argue for he clearly knew the truth. I began to suspect that during the night an angel might have visited him, and informed him of the diabolical menace he had on the altar. After a couple of minutes he let go of my chin, took me by the hair and drew my face closer to his. "I had three good women of this parish," he said bitterly, "who went to all the bother to take a taxi, and come to my house in the Moy, to tell me about the kind of villains that I have serving Mass. Now what do you think of that?"

I didn't really know what to think of it, but at least I was slightly relieved that his informants did not originate from a supernatural source. The thought flashed through my head that if some of the angels were so keen to change places with me, I would gladly welcome them in this situation. But that was clearly not going to happen, and I had to say something. "I'm sorry

Father," I spluttered, "I will never do anything like that again. I don't know what came over me."

The priest stared straight into my eyes, and I could see that there was still fire in his eyes. "You are a disgrace to the whole parish. You are a disgrace to the school and to Mr. Colgan here. You are a disgrace to your parents, who go to a lot of bother to see that you are well turned out for serving on the altar. Now, what will they think when they hear what you have been up to? I'm not looking forward, I can tell you, to going up to your house, to tell them the kind of ruffian they have reared."

My heart fell like a stone. It really felt like a big hard, cold lump in my chest. It was bad enough to have to go through this ordeal with strangers, but I dreaded to think of how I would face my parents. I knew how proud they were that their son had been picked for the altar, and I hated to think how I had disgraced them. I began to pray for some sudden bolt from heaven that would end my miserable life. At this critical point Mr. Colgan spoke for the first time. "The boy has done wrong Father but I am sure he has learned his lesson. Which of us can say that we have never made a mistake or done something we regret? I feel sure that if we leave it like this, we will never have any more bother with him. He's good here in school, and I am certain he will not let me down again. I think Father we should leave it at that."

Fr. Soraghan let go of my hair and looked from my face, up into that of the tall, solemn schoolmaster. He shook his head sadly, and stood looking from one of

The Glow of the Oil Lamp

us to the other for a few moments, without saying a word. Finally he looked sternly into my face again. "Your teacher is a very wise and good man," he said to me. "I hope that you appreciate the trust that he has in you. I do hope that you will never let him down again. Because of him I will let it drop there, and I will not go up to inform your parents of the dreadful things you did."

I heaved a deep sigh of relief. The priest turned and lifted the sweeping brush, which had been leaning against the wall beside him. Holding the brush horizontally across my eyes he asked, "Do you see this brush?"

"I do, Father."

"Do you see the shaft of this brush?"

"I do, Father."

"Do you see how thick the shaft of this brush is?"

"I do, Father."

"Well, if I ever hear of you misbehaving on the altar again, I'll break the shaft of this brush across your back. Now, do you know what I have said?"

"I do, Father."

"Are you sure you have understood what I have said?"

"I am, Father."

The priest was still looking into my eyes, and I could see that the anger had faded from his. He glanced upwards at Mr.Colgan, and then he looked back at me. "I hope you are keeping up the practice at the football," he said softly. "Mr.Colgan tells me that you are the best in the school at the minute. That's good. Now off you go and get your lunch."

I could hardly see the door at the far side of the room. When I did manage to cross the floor on wobbly legs, I could hardly turn the handle, but when I did manage it, I was hit by the sweet taste of fresh air, and an overwhelming sense of relief. In the playground, half the school gathered round to hear what had transpired, but I was so tense and faint that I mumbled only a few words to inform them that it was none of their business. That was the one lunchtime when I was unable or unwilling to play football. From that day on as well, my behaviour round the altar improved greatly, even though I cannot claim that it was for religious reasons.

In the weeks and months and years that followed Fr.Soraghan never mentioned the incident again, even though I would meet him two or three times a week. And Mr. Colgan behaved as though it has never taken place. Apparently the three ladies hired the taxi again, and arrived in great annoyance at Fr.Soraghan's house, to enquire why such a ruffian was still serving Mass. They were told to go home and look after their husbands and families, and if they did that they would be fully occupied, and not have time to mind other people's business. A son of one of the women was in my class, and told the story in school. No word of it ever reached my parents for they never mentioned it.

Having been an exceptional athlete himself, Fr.Soraghan took a great interest in all the sporting activities in the parish. He had a habit of managing to arrive in the village at lunch time, and would immediately be mobbed by hoards of youngsters, for he was always loaded with sweets, which he distributed freely to all around him. He would usually spend some time watching the boys playing football, but his great love was camogie, and he spent all his free time training the girls, so that many of his teams won county championships.

Every year he picked three or four girls, who were his best players, to take on a trip to the south of Ireland. One year, when I was nine, he chose two altar boys from our side of the parish, and two from the Moy, and four camogie girls, and he informed us that he was taking us on a three day trip to Dublin. My mother was very excited and elated that the parish priest had chosen me to go on one of his expeditions. She made sure that I had all the clothes necessary, and especially a new pair of pyjamas. It was the first time in my life that I had ever seen this particular form of night attire.

My mother walked with me to Benburb, carrying my little case, and the priest collected me in the village for the long, exciting journey to Ireland's capital city. I was looking forward to seeing many of the towns along the way, for at that time, we had to learn off all the chief towns of each of the thirty two counties, and many of them attained a mystical significance in my imagination. I was the last of the load to be collected, and having waved good bye to my mother, the nine of us set off, crammed together in Fr. Soraghan's little Austin seven car, which was suitably named a matchbox.

We were all very excited as we made our slow way southward. There were still very few cars on the roads and it was a rare event to get a ride in one. It was a unique experience to be taken on a journey of a hundred miles. Fr. Soraghan gave us a running historical comment on the countryside as we travelled. I remember being very impressed with the size of Newry, which was probably the biggest town I had seen up till that time.

Our first stop was the impressive town of Dundalk. Here Fr. Soraghan's sister, Lucy, ran a big confectionery shop, and the priest cleared a good part of her shelves with the stock of sweets and drinks that he bought for his guests. The others were spellbound by the sight of all the sweets, but I had the advantage of having been the friend of American soldiers, so perhaps it made less of an impact on me. As we were driving out of Dundalk, I could not help asking, "Do we go by Ardee, Father?"

The priest gave a sudden start. He turned round to look at me, so that the car slewed to the left, and we nearly crashed into the footpath. "What was that you said?" he asked, and I thought there was an edge to his voice, and I wondered what I had done wrong.

"I was just asking you if we were going through Ardee, Father," I answered in as quiet and respectful a tone as I could muster.

"And why did you want to go by Ardee?" This time his voice was normal and he kept his eyes on the road.

"Well, I thought it would be nice to see the place where Cuhullain and his best friend fought their great battle, Father." I was praying earnestly that my words did not sound too cheeky or that he might think that I was telling him which way to go.

The Glow of the Oil Lamp

"Oh, I suppose Billy Colgan has been telling you about the legends of Ireland. I suppose he has told you all about the cattle raid of Cooley. We have been passing through Cooley since we left Newry you know, and this is my country; this is the place where I was born and reared. I am very proud of this part of Ireland. Now what did Billy tell you about the battle?"

"It wasn't Mr. Colgan who told me, Father; it was my father."

Again the priest gave a jump, he looked round at me, and again the car slewed across the road, this time heading for the right hand side. Just in time he managed to get control and continued his driving. After a couple of minute's silence, he asked, "But sure your father is only a labourer. How does he know about all these things?"

This was a sore point. I had convinced the boys in school that we had a horse, that we were farmers, and if the story got out that I was telling lies, I did not fancy the consequences on my reputation. I took time to think before I answered, and regretted that I had opened my big mouth in the first place. I remembered Da warning me that I had only one mouth, but two ears, and it was a good idea to keep the mouth shut and the ears open.

"Yes, Father, Da does work away from home a lot. But he is a farmer as well you know." This was a gross exaggeration but I hoped to get away with it. The priest slowed the car till we were nearly stopped. He was obviously thinking. Finally driving more normally, and looking straight ahead he asked, "And did he tell you anything about the next big town we're coming to? It's called Drogheda."

I was now feeling quite uneasy. I wished that he would ask some of the others about these things. I could not work out why he was so intent on picking on me. "Well, Father, I think that he said Oliver Plunkett's head was there, and he told me about how the two kings fought the battle of the Boyne there, and how Billy won it."

"Did he say anything about how that battle might affect you?" the priest asked.

This seemed to me to be a very strange question. For the life of me I could not work out where all this was leading, and I wished he would leave me alone to look at the scenery. I knew the battle had taken place a very long time ago and I could not see any way in which it would affect me. "He told me the story of the ferryman, Father."

Again the priest gave a start but this time the car stayed on course. "And how might the story of the ferryman go?" He asked the question while glancing over his shoulder to look into my face.

I was now getting really worried and annoyed. I had been looking forward to the trip a lot, but now I began to wish that I had been left at home. I wished fervently that I had never mentioned Ardee, and that I had taken my father's advice and kept my mouth closed. I sat thinking for quite a few moments. "What's this about the ferryman?" repeated the priest, clearly determined to get an answer.

"Da says, Father, that on the day before the battle, king Billy came down to see what all the land was like along the river. He had examined all the land on the north side, and he wanted to do the same on the south. But there was no bridge at that time, and the river was deep, so that there was a problem about how to get across. There was a ferryman at that spot, who had a wee rowing boat, and the king paid this man to take him across. Half way across the river the ferryman stopped rowing, and turned to the king and asked, "Your Majesty, who is going to win the battle tomorrow?"

The king put his hand on the ferryman's shoulder and was quiet for a second or two. Then he said, "My good man, there is no need for you to worry about who will win the battle, because on the day after tomorrow you will still be rowing this wee boat."

Fr. Soraghan drove on, apparently deep in thought. It was quite a while before he asked, "And do you understand the meaning of the lesson that is in that story, Arthur?" This time I answered fairly quickly, "No, Father, but Dad said to remember the story and when I was older, it might come in useful to me."

"I think that is very good advice," he replied and to my great relief started to show us places along the road where he had won high jumps, or races, and other places where great camogie teams came from. The attention was taken away from me, and I lay back at ease, hoping that no more notice would be taken of me. To my great delight, we reached Dublin, and no one spoke to me in the meantime.

The Glow of the Oil Lamp

Darkness was beginning to fall as we came into the capital city. Fr. Soraghan installed us in the hotel St.George, which was just off Parnell Square, and very near to O'Connell Street. We were given rooms in an annex at the back, the boys on one floor, and the girls on another, but we seemed to have the place to ourselves. We had a meal and a chat, and apart from getting a look at the city after dark, the first day of our trip was over.

After breakfast next morning, Fr. Soraghan appeared, and after a short talk with us, he gave us money to get sweets and any other things that we might want. He told us we were free to come and go as we wished, but warned us not to steal things out of the shops. If we wanted something, and we did not have enough money to buy it, we were to ask him. Looking back on that episode today, I find it hard to believe that anyone would leave a group of children from the country, free to roam around Dublin as they wished, especially since not one of us had ever been away from home before. But that is exactly what this simple priest did. It must have been what he had been doing for years, and no one was ever any the worse for it. Maybe he was just plain lucky, or maybe he had a guarantee of protection from above. Certainly, had any of our parents known the extent to which we were trusted, not one of us would have been in Dublin.

I have a very hazy memory of the events during the time we spent in the city, except for one incident. In the afternoon of the second day, we decided to climb Nelson's pillar, which was at that time, the most notable landmark in O'Connell Street. We paid our entry fee and made our way up the spiral staircase, to the gallery at the top, which was protected by a fairly high iron railing. From the top of the pillar we had a wonderful panoramic view of the city, which reminded me of the view of the countryside from the fort above my home. I remember gazing down on people in the street below and being very surprised, because from that height, they looked like so many little black crows.

Someone, or perhaps all of us, had bought big sticks of Dublin rock in one of the shops. We began to throw the rock down to see what effect its landing on the street, would have on the people below. Fortunately it did not hit anyone, but when it landed and smashed on the road or footpath, people ran towards the spot to examine this material, that had dropped out of the sky. We all howled with laughter at the sight of the little black dots all converging, to see what was happening. The guard caught on to what we had been doing and chased us, scolding about barbarians from the country who should not be allowed into civilized society. He demanded to talk to our parents, and it took a long time to convince him that they were a hundred miles away. I am not sure if the poor man feared an invasion of our like, some of whom might actually manage to murder one of the citizens.

On our way home from Dublin, Fr.Soraghan decided to go by the Slane road so that I could go through Ardee. He showed us the hill of Tara, where the high kings used to live, and told us how St. Patrick had lit a famous fire on the hill of Slane. When we got to Ardee, we stopped on a bridge, and he explained how we were standing

The Glow of the Oil Lamp

on the very spot where Cuhullain and Ferdiagh fought their famous battle. He asked me not to forget to tell my father, that we had stopped there, and that the town's name means the ford of Ferdiagh. We arrived home in the late evening of the third day, happy and safe, and thankfully no one had died or was injured as a result of my first sally outside the parish of my birth.

CHAPTER 21
THE FADING GLOW

When I went back to school after the long summer holidays in 1948, I was looking forward to leaving school in a couple of year's time. The leaving age at that time was fourteen, and that seemed within easy reach. It was somewhat of a surprise, therefore, when Mr. Colgan increased my nightly homework and demanded very high standards of tidiness and presentation from me. A new boy, called Mick McKeever, had come to the school about a year before, and much the same was expected from him. It was only on a very odd night now, that we would have visitors, and in the long winter nights, I found the extra work useful for passing the time. Oil lamps had been discarded for tilleys in most of the neighbouring houses, but my mother bought an Aladdin lamp, which had a much bigger mantle, did not make noise, and gave a very good light. I worked away on the kitchen table while my parents read, knitted or talked quietly by the fire.

I had quite a bit of reading to do and lots of complex comprehension questions to answer, and at least once a week the master gave me an essay to write. For quite a

The Glow of the Oil Lamp

while I had loved reading and had walked every Saturday to the Moy for my supply of comics. Having given me a couple of packets of steel nibs and blotting paper, Mr. Colgan expected the work to be presented without a single blot, and in clear, careful handwriting. Mick and I found ourselves kept in school for an extra half hour in the evenings too, and this was a lot more irritating. The parsing and analysis had become so advanced that it usually took the double page of an exercise book to set it out. There were a few times when Mr. Colgan took the work home with him, in order to work out, if I had got it right.

Arithmetic involved the solving of quite difficult problems. There were trains, which left far away places like Moscow and had a thousand miles to go to Paris. Others travelled in the opposite direction but at a different speed, and left at a different time. I had to work out where they would pass each other, and at what time each would arrive at its destination. Mick was excellent at the arithmetic but not quite so good at the English. I remember one particular time when I had spent a very long time the previous night, working on a sum, which took up a page and a half. Next day the master marked it wrong, working from the answer book. Mick got it right and Mr. Colgan told me to take it home and work out where I had gone wrong. He told me what the answer should be. I worked at it for over an hour, but I could not come up with the right answer.

Next morning I brought it up to him and told him my problem. He looked through it but could not see where I had gone wrong. He called Mick up and had a look at his work. "How did you get this answer? he asked him. "I worked it out Sir, like all the rest," replied Mick. Mr. Colgan told him to go and bring up his schoolbag. He searched in the bag and threw an answer book out on the desk. "So you went and bought an answer book, Mick," he said quietly. "If I had known that you wanted the answers I would have given them to you and saved you the money. The answers are not important; it's you knowing how to get them, that is. You are fooling no one only yourself. It so happens that this answer in the book is wrong, it's a misprint, but I hope you both learn a lot from this." I am sure that we both did.

Problems about tanks were a big part of the work we did. They were strange tanks, which had pipes feeding in water at the top and other pipes of a different size, taking the water out at the bottom. We had to work out how long it would take to fill the tanks to a certain height, or indeed to empty them. Geometry and then algebra were part of our work too. My father, who was always very good at arithmetic, used to look at the work I was doing, and complain that he had never done anything like that at school. He had always claimed that his old school master, a man called Duffy, was a great teacher, and it surprised me to hear him admit that he thought Mr. Colgan was even better.

All this work was fine in the long, dark nights of winter, but as the days lengthened it was not so attractive. Mr. Colgan, however, eased off on the written work and gave me lots of books to read and I did not mind that at all. He produced a little Irish text book and started to teach me a few sentences in that language. I was to discover later that the book was in southern Irish, and I have wondered since, if he knew much about the language himself. I was really puzzled as to why all this was taking place and some of my friends felt sorry for me, and thought I was being picked upon. They said they would not like to change places with me. One day I asked Mr. Colgan why I was getting all the extra work. He laughed and said that in the previous very bad winter, I had only been at school for one or two days each week and he was making up for lost time.

I was about to go home as usual one evening in the springtime, when Mr. Colgan took a letter out of his desk drawer and asked me to bring it home, and get my parents to sign it. He told me that it was an application form to sit the entrance examination for Saint Patrick's College in Armagh. Even if they did not wish me to go there, he wanted me to sit the examination. I produced the form at home and my mother could not believe her eyes. She was truly delighted. She said that if I passed the examination, she would send me as a boarder, no matter what it cost, and my father agreed. They filled in the form and sent a letter to Mr. Colgan, outlining their plans and thanking him for giving me the chance.

I had heard of only one boy who had gone to the college or indeed to any secondary school. This was Frank, the son of our next door neighbour, Barney Conlon. I knew that the Conlons were all very clever people and their son would be expected to do well, wherever he went. His two sisters had gone to secondary school too, but they had to cycle to Dungannon. Maureen, the elder of the two, was the only person that I had ever heard of, who had gone to The Queen's University of Belfast and got a good degree. I did not know what this meant but saw it as a passport into a world, which I would never know.

Frank had been quite a celebrity in the area about twelve years before, when he did his senior examination and won the King's scholarship, which at that time entitled him to train as a teacher. In the early part of that year the Education Committee of Dungannon Council, which was in control of our area, announced that they would give a full scholarship to anyone who reached the required standard. Frank's results were far above the standard, but realising that he was not a Unionist, the Committee announced that they had no money for the scholarship, and turned down his application. Barney had never been known to avoid a fight, and he took his case to higher authorities. A relation of Mrs Conlon's, a man called M.J.Kelly, had a sister married to the Lord Mayor of Dublin, and was himself a wealthy and powerful man in Dublin and promised to take the case to the highest court in the land. Word of the dispute reached Stormont, and the Minister of Education informed the Committee in Dungannon that they had no option but to pay the scholarship.

It had taken quite a while to reach this stage, however, and Frank was two months late for his course. He had obtained a post in Radio Eireann, and in a short time became a well known broadcaster in the Irish language using the Irish version of his name, Proinsias O'Conluain. The case was dropped, but Barney felt that he had proved his point and that in future no one

The Glow of the Oil Lamp

could be denied a scholarship because they were not Unionists. This was proven the following year, when Maureen won a scholarship to Queen's, and it was never questioned.

On a fine Saturday morning in the springtime, my mother got me suitably dressed, and I set out on my bicycle for Armagh. Mr. Colgan had told me that the college was to the right of the cathedral and that I could not miss it. I dismounted at the cathedral gates and wheeled my bicycle up a narrow path, which led to the college. I was about to park it against a neat hedge, when a man shouted at me, and came towards me. "What do you think you're doing, leaving that bicycle there?" he asked in an angry tone. "I have to do an exam here this morning," I answered, "and I was leaving it here until I come out again."

"Well, you're not leaving that thing on my newly cut hedge." he said. "Take it and leave it away in that corner, down by the handball alleys." He pointed down another path, which went off at right angles and having got rid of my bicycle I stood gazing in wonder at the huge walls, which he called handball alleys. The man had come with me and he must have seen the wonder in my eyes. "Where do you come from anyway?," he asked, "I can see that you have never seen handball alleys before."

"I come from Sessiagh." I told him.

"And where the hell might that be?" he asked, "And what school do you go to at home?"

"I go to Blackwatertown, and my teacher is a Mr. Colgan." I answered.

"Oh, I know Billy Colgan for he lives in the town here. But what the hell are you doing here this morning?"

"I came in to do the exam."

The man took a sideways look at me and gave a snort of a laugh. "And what the hell is the likes of you doing the exam for? There's boys here from the best schools in the town, and from Dungannon and from Cookstown and from Portadown and from all over the north of Ireland. There will be over three hundred boys sitting the exam this morning, and the same next Saturday morning. You haven't a chance in hell."

"I know that," I answered calmly, for he had not told me anything that surprised me, except that I had not been expecting such a huge number of people to be taking the examination.

By now there were big crowds of boys arriving at the college. Some came on foot and followed the little path, which I had used. But the great majority were arriving in cars, obviously accompanied by their parents. It struck me that I was in amongst the rich folk, and I felt totally out of place. However, I had come this far and there was little option but to follow the crowd into the big building, and up to a huge hall full of desks, which someone told me was called the study hall. A priest at the door told me I would find my desk near the front, for they were named in alphabetical order.

The examination lasted two and a half hours. I found all the things on it that Mr. Colgan had been doing with me. I could not believe it when I saw the sentence for parsing and analysis. I had not met anything as easy for well over a year. The comprehension was not bad either and the essay was on a harvest day, so that suited me too. The arithmetic was easier than I had been used to as well. I felt perfectly relaxed for I knew I had no chance against all this brilliant opposition, so there was no point in getting worried.

My parents asked me how things went when I got home. I told them that there were six hundred boys doing the exam, and that the most of them seemed to be very posh people, and that I had no chance of passing the test. On Monday the same conversation took place with Mr.Colgan, who had got a copy of the papers, and asked me about every section in detail. "So you saw a big crowd of very rich people," he said. "I hope you didn't get the idea that they were better than you, just because they had cars. And I know that man you were talking to. His name is Tommy McGinn and he is the caretaker at the college, and I thought he would have more sense. All I'll say to you is, don't let appearances fool you. We'll wait and see what happens."

It was coming into the good weather and to my delight the homework almost disappeared. I was expected to learn a couple of sentences in Irish each night but otherwise I was free to practice football and to run with my hoop round the fields to my heart's content. A few weeks went past and one morning the postman called, and gave my mother a big letter in a brown envelope. I had passed the exam, and the letter gave details of all the things I would need to board at the college. Football boots and a strip for physical education excited me, while I felt very guilty that my mother had to find the money for lots of new clothes.

The Glow of the Oil Lamp

I enjoyed the holidays that summer but I was looking forward to going into this new life and I found the time somewhat long.

About a fortnight after it was decided that I would be going to the college, Fr. Moore called at our house one evening. He told my parents that he was delighted with the news, and that he would be talking to Fr. Sherridan, the President, and he would put in a good word for me and tell him that I was one of his altar boys. Fr. Moore had been in the same class at school as my father, and they had been friends ever since. The priest spoke in beautifully cultured English and it surprised me when Da told me that when he was at school he had a very bad stoppage and found it hard to speak at all. This visit was unusual, in that he found my father at home, whereas he would normally be away at work if a priest called.

"It's a long time since we sat together in Eglish school, Mick," he said, with a smile at my father, "You would hardly have thought at that time that one of us would end up as parish priest to the other. Haven't I done well?"

My father looked at him and answered with more of a laugh than a smile, "Indeed Peter Moore, it is no surprise to me. I can remember you being left to school in a fancy pony and trap, when the rest of us had to come in our bare feet. And I suppose you forget that I used to have to do your sums for you, because at that time, you weren't all that bright. But the Moores always had the money. There's not a doubt that if I had had

The Glow of the Oil Lamp

your chances, I'd be sitting in Armagh today, with the red hat on me."

Fr. Moore got up, said goodbye to everyone, and went out to his car, shaking his head and laughing.

In the late afternoon of the first Sunday in September everything was ready and a taxi was ordered to take my mother, myself, and my cases, to Armagh. It so happened that Frank Conlon was at home that day and he called round to wish me well, since I was following in his footsteps. I remember saying to him, "My uncle Pat was fooling me the other day, and he said that the only time the boys get a fry is on Saint Patrick's day. He must think I am an awful fool." Frank looked at me and smiled. "I'm sorry to tell you," he said, "that your uncle Pat was telling you the truth. I'm afraid the food is not good. It may be better now than when I was there, but you only get bacon and eggs on Saint Patrick's day. But you'll survive, you'll see."

We arrived at the college somewhat early, because my mother had to meet Fr. Sherridan, the President of the college. The tallish priest had sleeked back silver hair and he was very formal. I knew immediately that this man would take no prisoners. I knew that I would have to do exactly what he demanded or I would be out. Having shaken hands with the two of us he said, "Mrs Daly, I want a few words with you. The boy can find his own way from here. Go through that door boy, on your right, and find your way up to your dormitory." My mother said a quick farewell to me and had no option but to leave me to find my way. Parents were

The Glow of the Oil Lamp

not allowed beyond the big doors, which separated the foyer from the rest of the college.

As I opened the door Tommy McGinn was standing there with a brush in his hand. "Oh, so you're back," he said with a smile, "you must have done well in the test. What place did you get?" The places were given on the report, so I was able to tell him I had got ninth. "Be God, boy, that is very good," he said. "You'll be in the twos, which is the top class in your year, and I hope you do well. Go up those stairs on your left there and on the top floor you'll find your dorm. All the best now lad, and if ever there is anything I can do for you, don't be afraid to ask."

The huge door swung shut behind me, cutting me off from the world I had so far known. When I would leave this place in five year's time, the glow of the oil lamp would have faded forever from the place where I had spent a happy childhood.

The author's father, Michael Daly, more commonly known as Mick Dawley of Sessiagh. Perhaps his wisdom was not always appreciated in childhood but it certainly has been in later years.

THE CORNCRAKE'S CALL

Dear father I'm taking the pen in my hand
To tell you how everything's changed in the land.
In big swanky houses we're living in style
But they've wrecked and they've poisoned this beautiful isle.
You remember how the corncrake in the meadow would call,
Now the nearest you'll find one is in west Donegal,
Oh t'was grand when my mammy would bring us the tae
And when you did the pitching and I built the hay.

Some people sit silent half the day and all night,
Sure I'm thankful to God when they put out the light.
On a box in the corner, it's pictures they watch
If you're lucky and patient, a few words you might snatch.
You know how the neighbours in the wee house would call
And they'd tell all their stories, the big and the small,
Oh t'was grand when my mammy would get up and say,
"Sure there's new griddle bread for a wee drop of tae."

You'll remember the planting where the wild woodcock lay,
How the larks in the springtime made their nests in the hay.
Well now they cut silage, and foul slurry they spread,
The larks' nests are ruined, and the woodcock are dead.

The Glow of the Oil Lamp

And sometimes you taught me in the brook to catch trout,
With the skill of your hands you could fetch the fish out.
Oh t'was grand when the sun made the pure waters gleam,
Now the factories and farmers have polluted the stream.

I can still feel my feet on the new stubbled sod,
When you cut the corn and I held the rod.
The new yankee scythe o'er your shoulder you'd heel,
And the stone made fine music as you honed the fine steel.
But now there's big combines in the fields all around
And in ten dusty minutes they cut an acre of ground,
But for all their great power sure they blight each new dawn
For the scythe, like you father, is buried and gone.

Each evening you'd loose out the horse to be fed,
And I rode on his back while you walked at his head,
And although I'm gone sixty, I can still feel his sweat,
And my heart feels so heavy and my eyes they are wet.
For I still see his collar where it hung on the jam,
And the pig that we'd killed for its bacon and ham.
How you walked from your work, and I sat on your head,
And the sweet air was scented with mother's baked bread.

Oh goodbye to you father, for I still could go on,
About things of the past, and the days that are gone.
But it's well to be you that has had your long day,
When we worked with the horse, with the fork made the hay.
And we kept the best straw for to mend the old thatch.
Whereas now on our trousers, you'd ne'er see a patch.
Oh it's now that I'm thinking, I'll see you ere long,
Where there's fish in the streams and the lark's still in song.

ISBN 1412024285